The
COMPANIONS *in Christ*™
Network

www.companionsinchrist.org

So much more!

Companions in Christ is *so much more* than printed resources.
It offers an ongoing LEADERSHIP NETWORK that provides:

➢ Opportunities to connect with other small groups who are also journeying through the *Companions in Christ* series.

➢ Insights and testimonies from other *Companions in Christ* participants

➢ An online discussion room where you can share or gather information

➢ Training opportunities that develop and deepen the leadership skills used in formational groups

➢ Helpful leadership tips and articles as well as updated lists of supplemental resources

Just complete this form and drop it in the mail, and you can enjoy the many benefits available through the *Companions in Christ* NETWORK! Or, enter your contact information at www.companionsinchrist.org/leaders.

Name: _____

Address: _____

City/State/Zip: _____

Church: _____

Email: _____

Phone: _____

COMPANIONS *in Christ*™
Upper Room Ministries
PO Box 340012
Nashville, TN 37203-9540

The COMPANIONS *in Christ* Series

The Way of Transforming Discipleship

PARTICIPANT'S BOOK

Trevor Hudson
Stephen D. Bryant

UPPER
ROOM BOOKS®
NASHVILLE

Cover design: Left Coast Design, Portland, OR
Cover art: Stephan Daigle, "Three Crosses/Landscape"
Interior art flap: The Metropolitan Museum of Art, Wrightsman Fund, 2004
Photograph © 2004 The Metropolitan Museum of Art

Interior design and implementation: Nancy Cole-Hatcher
Second printing: 2008

Library of Congress Cataloging-in-Publication Data

Hudson, Trevor, 1951–
    Companions in Christ : the way of transforming discipleship participant's book / Trevor Hudson, Stephen D. Bryant.
        p. cm.
    ISBN 978-0-8358-9842-3
    1. Discipling (Christianity) 2. Spiritual formation. I. Bryant. Stephen D. II. Title.
BV4520.H765 2005
253'.7—dc22   2005026286

Printed in the United States of America

**For more information on *Companions in Christ*
call 1-800-972-0433 or visit www.companionsinchrist.org**

Contents

Acknowledgments

*T*he original twenty-eight-week *Companions in Christ* resource grew from the seeds of a vision long held by Stephen D. Bryant, editor and publisher of Upper Room Ministries, and given shape by Marjorie J. Thompson, director of Upper Room's Pathways in Congregational Spirituality and spiritual director to *Companions in Christ.* The vision, which has now expanded into the Companions in Christ series, was realized through the efforts of many people over many years. The original advisers, consultants, authors, editors, and test churches are acknowledged in the foundational resource. We continue to be grateful to each person and congregation named.

The Way of Transforming Discipleship is the sixth title in the series building on the foundation of *Companions in Christ.* Like its predecessors, it represents a shorter small-group resource intended to expand on the experience of participation in the twenty-eight-week *Companions* resource. However, a group may use this study prior to experiencing the *Companions in Christ* resource. The articles in the Participant's Book are adapted from sermons by Trevor Hudson. The daily exercises in the Participant's Book and the Deeper Explorations in the Leader's Guide are primarily the work of Stephen Bryant. We are grateful to Eileen Campbell-Reed for so carefully editing the materials and for writing the closing retreat. Thanks also to Sally Havens and Zena Smith for helping us review and test the material. The staff team who worked on this resource included Robin Pippin, Kathleen Stephens, Janice Neely, Rita Collett, Lynne Deming, Marjorie J. Thompson, and Stephen D. Bryant.

Preface

*I*n late 2001 Upper Room Ministries responded to an invitation from leaders in the Methodist Church of Southern Africa to assist them in developing Christian spirituality resources for a post-apartheid era. We asked the question, "Who in southern Africa represents and articulates the authentic Christian spirituality we are talking about?" Again and again, a name that surfaced in response was Trevor Hudson.

Since then, Upper Room Ministries has come to know Trevor Hudson as one of God's great gifts to the ecumenical church. He stands alongside Desmond Tutu, Peter Storey, and others whose leadership for the church has been shaped in the crucible of southern African experience in recent years. Trevor is an author, having published several excellent and helpful books in the area of Christian spirituality. He is a pastor, deeply committed to the spiritual care of the people of Northfield Methodist Church in Benoni, just outside Johannesburg. He is also a teacher, spiritual guide, and retreat leader who in the 1980s and 1990s led groups of white Christians on "pilgrimages of pain and hope" in which they trespassed the racial boundaries of apartheid and spent days living with the invisible poor of their own land, "listening to the groans" of humanity and of God.

Beneath the accolades, Trevor Hudson is a "Christ-follower" (to use his term), a humble man on a lifelong journey into the compassionate heart of God. In *The Way of Transforming Discipleship*, Trevor invites us to join him on that journey.

The material in this resource is based on a series of five outstanding messages that Trevor delivered in 2004 at SOUL*feast*, Upper Room Ministries's summer conference on spiritual formation. (See www.upperroom.org/soulfeast for information.) At that event, Trevor guided us on a five-day pilgrimage "in search of an authentic Christian spirituality." Our minds and hearts were opened to a new vision in the course of exploring who we are in God, changing from the inside, listening to the groans, sharing in the healing grace of Jesus, and rediscovering Christian community together. Because the conference so transformed those who gathered that summer, we felt called to make Trevor's contribution accessible, not as another book to read but in the form of a small-group journey. It is our deep desire that this resource will inspire many more people in churches everywhere to seek a deeper life with God as Christ-followers in the world.

—Stephen D. Bryant

Introduction

Welcome to *Companions in Christ: The Way of Transforming Discipleship*, a small-group resource designed to help your small group explore and experience central elements in the journey of discipleship that follows the way of Jesus Christ. The aspects of discipleship that this resource explores include grounding our identity in our God-given belovedness, being mentored by Jesus Christ to befriend all of his followers, listening to the deep cries of pain and hope in our lives and in creation, experiencing the healing presence of God, and discovering genuine Christian community.

In response to the desire of many small groups to continue exploring spiritual practices that began with the original twenty-eight-week *Companions in Christ* resource, The Upper Room has developed the Companions in Christ series. *The Way of Transforming Discipleship* is the sixth title in the series. It offers a six-week journey (including a preparatory meeting) plus a Closing Pilgrimage and Retreat through which we hope to experience more deeply what it means to live as a Christ-follower. Previous titles in the Companions series include *The Way of Forgiveness*, an eight-week journey through the forgiven and forgiving life; *The Way of Blessedness*, a nine-week journey through the Beatitudes; *The Way of Grace*, a nine-week journey through central stories in the Gospel of John about encounters with Jesus; and *Exploring the Way*, a six-week introduction to the Christian spiritual journey.

With the exception of *Exploring the Way*, each resource in the

Companions series expands the foundational content of the twenty-eight-week resource and uses the same basic format. In *Companions in Christ* we explored the Christian spiritual life under five headings: Journey, Scripture, Prayer, Call, and Spiritual Guidance. Each supplementary volume explores in greater depth some aspect of one of these five areas of spiritual life and practice. *The Way of Transforming Discipleship* falls under the general heading of Journey, as it is an invitation to embrace the journey and enter into the lifelong practice of Christian discipleship.

As Christ-followers, our journeys always remain rooted in a biblical understanding of our faith. When we ponder Bible stories in a Companions group, we engage the stories as much as possible with our whole self. We want to include intellect, feeling, intuition, and will as we draw on classic practices of scriptural meditation and prayer. It is important to understand that Companions does not offer Bible study in any traditional sense. It represents a more experiential, formational approach to scripture than an informational approach.

Like the original *Companions in Christ* resource, *The Way of Transforming Discipleship* will help you deepen essential practices of the Christian life. It focuses on your daily experience of God and your growing capacity to respond to grace with gratitude, trust, love, and self-offering. Because this exploration takes place in the midst of a small group, you can expect increasingly to realize the blessings of mutual support, encouragement, guidance, and accountability in Christian community. Your growth in faith and maturation in spirit will benefit your congregation as well.

About the Resource and Process

Like all Companions resources, *The Way of Transforming Discipleship* has two primary components: individual reading and daily exercises throughout the week with this Participant's Book and a weekly two-hour meeting based on directions in the Leader's Guide.

Each weekly chapter in the Participant's Book introduces new material and provides five daily exercises to help you reflect on your life in light of the chapter content. After the Preparatory Meeting of your group, you will begin a weekly cycle as follows: On day 1 you will be asked to read the article; on days 2–6 you will complete each of the five daily exercises (found at the end of each week's reading); on day 7 you will meet with your group. An added feature of *The Way of Transforming Discipleship* is a week of daily exercises in preparation for the Closing Pilgrimage and Retreat.

The daily exercises aim to help you move from *information* (knowledge about) to *experience* (knowledge of). The time commitment for one daily exercise is approximately thirty minutes. An important part of this process involves keeping a personal notebook or journal in which you record reflections, prayers, and questions for later review and for reference at the weekly group meeting.

Weekly meetings include time for sharing reflections on the exercises of the past week and for moving deeper into the content of the article through various learning and prayer experiences. Meetings begin and end with simple worship times. You will need to bring your Participant's Book, your Bible, and your personal notebook or journal to each weekly group meeting. An annotated resource list on pages 83–89 describes additional book titles related to the weekly themes.

The Companions in Christ Network

An additional dimension of resources in the Companions series is the Network. The Network provides opportunities for you to share conversation and information. The Companions web site, www.companionsinchrist.org, includes a discussion room where you can offer insights, voice questions, and respond to others in an ongoing process of shared learning. The site provides a list of other Companions groups journeying through each of the resources in the series and their geographical locations so that you can make connections as you feel led. Connecting in these ways will enrich your group's experience and the experience of those to whom you reach out. It will help you become aware of the wider reality of our companionship in the body of Christ across geographic and denominational lines.

Your Personal Notebook or Journal

Keeping a journal or notebook (commonly called journaling) will be one of the most important dimensions of your personal experience with *The Way of Transforming Discipleship.* The Participant's Book gives you daily spiritual exercises each week. More often than not, you will be asked to note your thoughts, reflections, questions, feelings, or prayers in relation to the exercise. Upper Room Books has made available a Journal that you may purchase. You will want, at minimum, something more permanent than a ring binder or paper pad.

You may find that this kind of personal writing quickly becomes second nature. Your thoughts may start to pour out of you, giving expression to an inner life that has never been released. If, on the other hand, you find the writing difficult or cumbersome, give yourself permission to try it in a new way. A journal is for your eyes only, so you may choose any style that suits you. You need not worry about beautiful words, good grammar, spelling, or even complete sentences. Jotting down key ideas, insights, or musings in a few words or phrases works just fine. You might doodle while you think or sketch an image that comes to you. Make journaling fun and relaxed! Remember, you have complete freedom to share with the group only what you choose of your reflections.

Keeping a journal as you move through *The Way of Transforming Discipleship* is important for two reasons. First, the process of writing down thoughts clarifies them for us. Sometimes we really do not know what we think until we see our thoughts on paper, and often the process of writing generates new insight. Second, this personal record captures our inward experience over time so we can track changes in our thinking and growth. Memories are notoriously fragile and fleeting; specific feelings or creative connections we had two weeks ago or even three days ago can be hard to recall without a written record. Though your journal cannot capture all that goes through your mind in a single reflection period, it will offer reminders you draw on during small-group meetings each week.

When you begin a daily exercise, have your journal and pen at hand. You need not wait until you have finished thinking an exercise through. Learn to stop and write as you go. Think on paper. Feel free to write anything that comes to you. Even ideas that seem off the topic may turn out to be more relevant than you first believed. If the process seems clumsy at first, keep an open mind. Like any spiritual practice, it grows easier over time, and its value becomes more apparent.

Your weekly practice of journaling is shaped as follows. On the first day after your group meeting, read the next week's article. Jot down your responses: "aha" moments, questions, points of disagreement, images, or any other reflections you wish to record. You may prefer to note these in the margins of the Participant's Book. Over the next five days, you will do the exercises for the week, recording responses as they are invited. On the day of the group meeting, it will help to review what you have written through the week, perhaps marking portions you would like to share in the group. Bring your journal with you to meetings so you can refer to it directly or refresh your memory about thoughts you want to paraphrase during discussion times. With time, you may find that journaling helps you to discern more clearly your own pattern of living and how God is at work in your life.

Your Group Meeting

The weekly meeting is divided into four segments. First you will gather for a brief time of worship and prayer, which allows you to set aside the concerns of the day and center on God's guiding presence as you begin the group session.

The second segment of the meeting is called "Sharing Insights." During this time the group leader will invite you to talk about your experiences with the daily exercises. The leader will participate as a member and share his or her responses as well. Generally each member will briefly share thoughts and insights related to specific exercises. This process helps participants learn and practice what it means to listen deeply. You are a community of persons seeking to listen to God and to one another so that you can live more faithfully as disciples of Christ. The group provides a supportive community to explore your listening, your spiritual practices, and your efforts to employ those practices in daily life.

This community does not function as a traditional support group where people are sometimes quick to offer advice or to comment on one another's experiences. In Companions groups, members try to honor one another's experiences through prayerful attentiveness, affirmation, and respectful clarifying questions. The "Sharing Insights" part of the meeting is less meaningful when persons interrupt and comment on what is being said or try to "fix" what they see as a problem (called "cross talk"). Group members are invited to trust the Holy Spirit's guidance and help one another listen to that guidance.

The "Sharing Insights" time presents a unique opportunity to learn how God works differently in each life. Our journeys, while varied, enrich others' experiences. Other people's faith stories allow us to see anew how God's activity touches or addresses our lives in unexpected ways. The group will need to establish some ground rules to facilitate this sharing. Participants need clearly to agree that each person will speak only about his or her own beliefs, feelings, and responses and that all group members have permission to share only what and when they are ready to share. Above all, the group should maintain confidentiality so that what is shared in the group stays in the group. Spouses or close friends in the same group will need to agree between themselves on permissible boundaries of confidentiality, so that the choice to reveal oneself does not inadvertently reveal intimacies to the group without the other's consent.

The leader participates in this sharing and aids the process by listening and summarizing key insights that have surfaced. The leader closes this part of the meeting by calling attention to any patterns or themes that seem to have emerged from the group sharing. These patterns may point to a word God is offering to the group.

The third segment of the meeting is called "Deeper Explorations." This part of the meeting gives group members an opportunity to explore a deeper dimension of God's grace, to practice related spiritual disciplines, or to explore implications of the week's theme for their church.

As it began, the group meeting ends with a brief time of worship. In this fourth segment members may lift to God the needs and concerns that emerge from the experience of the meeting itself or express the spiritual learning of the week through symbol, ritual, and prayer.

Invitation to the Journey

The weeks you give to *The Way of Transforming Discipleship* offer a unique opportunity to focus on your spiritual journey in relation to Jesus Christ and the world he came to redeem. In reflecting on each article and doing the daily exercises, you will explore your belovedness in God, changing from the inside out, listening to the groans of all creation, experiencing healing in God's presence, and knowing authentic Christian community. You will discover "signposts" along this Way that will guide you in responding to Christ's call to discipleship. Other members of your small group, your companions on the journey, will encourage your seeking and learning as you encourage theirs.

The life Jesus calls us to is truly a transformed life in which our mind, heart, and action reveal the beauty and wholeness of Christ's spirit in us. This is what it means to be conformed to the image of Christ, the goal of spiritual formation in the Christian tradition. It is a goal we can attain only as we walk through life alongside our Risen Lord, by the grace of the Holy Spirit. We open ourselves to this grace most readily through prayer, faith, love, authenticity, and a willingness to be vulnerable to the pain and hope of the world around us.

So we invite you to open yourself to the transformation God desires to bring about in you as you explore what it means to be a Christ-follower. Pray and claim boldly from God whatever you feel you need as you begin this small-group experience. May the the Holy Spirit guide your footsteps as you follow Jesus, walking in the light alongside your companions!

Preparatory Meeting
Becoming a Christ-Follower

I became a Christ-follower at the age of seventeen. The gracious invitation to "follow me," rooted in a great love that had sought me from my very beginnings, burned its way into my heart and evoked both desire and response. Ever since that moment of new beginning I have been learning from Jesus how to live the one life that I have been given. This search has connected me with the lives of many other seeking pilgrims along the Way. In recent years I have come to recognize this common seeking as a widespread yearning in the hearts of men and women for an authentic spirituality.

Spirituality is a slippery word. Some are suspicious of the term. For those whose daily lives revolve around frantic timetables of preparing breakfast, getting children to school on time, holding down a stressful eight-to-five job, paying monthly bills, and cleaning the house, *spirituality* sounds strange and impractical. It suggests another world of inactivity, passivity, and uninterrupted silences. For those whose life experiences have been scarred by suffering and oppression, the term often suggests escapism, indifference, and uninvolvement. Indeed, *spirituality* needs definition. Spirituality is being intentional about the development of those convictions, attitudes, and actions through which the Christ-following life is shaped and given personal expression within our everyday lives. In a nutshell, it is the way of transforming discipleship.

Amidst this widespread yearning for a vital and real spirituality we need to be discerning. Within contemporary Christian congregations some expressions of spirituality are foreign to the biblical tradition and

Our faith journey depends upon roads that transform us as we travel. . . . Roads that transform not only with challenges that enable us to do more work in God's name, but challenges that encourage us to become more of who God desires us to be.

—Luther E. Smith Jr.

unrelated to the spirit of the crucified and risen Lord. Some congregations are obsessively concerned with personal needs and have minimal concern for those who suffer. Some others frequently endorse a spirituality of social struggle and involvement that avoids the biblical imperative for personal conversion and transformation. Such endorsement falls victim to the dangerous illusion, alive and well in our midst, that we can build a more equitable, compassionate, and just society while we remain the same and continue life as usual.

In *The Way of Transforming Discipleship* I offer a number of signposts that lead us to the development of a renewed spirituality centered in the life of Jesus, our ever-present Savior and Lord. I am neither an academic theologian nor an expert in the area of spirituality. The words that I share were birthed amidst the daily tasks of washing dishes and being a parent; the vocational commitments of breaking bread, and supporting and encouraging people in their discipleship; and the continual challenges of a turbulent nation struggling to reconstruct itself along more democratic lines. Within these tasks, commitments, and crises, I have struggled, often unsuccessfully, to live an authentic Christ-following life. My words are shaped by these struggles.

Wherever you may find yourself along the Way, may you discover in these reflections some nourishing food for the journey. It is my hope that in offering these few signposts, all of us may become more radically open to the transformation that God is able to bring about in our personal and social lives. An authentic Christian spirituality always stretches toward the transforming of our personal lives and of the societies in which we live, work, and play. I will be immeasurably grateful if, in the lives of some fellow pilgrims and seekers, these signposts contribute to such a transformation.

As you gather each week you will be invited to take part in some Deeper Explorations, practices for a group to explore together. Community is both central and critical to the way of transforming discipleship. These practices assume that you have begun to engage with some of the issues raised in the articles. An instructive ancient proverb reads: "Hear and forget, see and remember, do and understand." As

The great call to the spiritual life amounts to little more than learning how to receive what first and finally can only come as gift, and then to live freely in and from that gift.

—Michael Downey

you read this material, I hope that your hearing will lead to seeing, and your seeing to doing, so that you will discover and participate in the way of transforming discipleship.

—Trevor Hudson

EXERCISE FOR REFLECTION

The life of Christian faith and discipleship is often portrayed as a journey, a pilgrimage, or simply as the Way. When you think back on your own life of faith, what signposts have marked the way for your journey? For example:

- When did you become a Christ-follower?
- Who is someone who influenced your journey?
- What events or experiences have prepared the way or opened the way for you?

God made us in order to use us, and use us in the most profitable way: for God's purpose, not ours. To live a spiritual life means subordinating all other interests to that single fact.
—Evelyn Underhill

Week 1
Knowing Who We Are

Read Matthew 3:13-17

One day seven-year-old Johnny asked his mom the question that parents dread: "Where did I come from?" His theologically astute mom answered, "Johnny, you came from dust, and one day you are going to return to dust." Fascinated by this, Johnny ran off to play, repeating in his head the mantra, "I came from dust, and one day I shall return to dust."

Later that day Johnny crawled under a bed into a space that had not been swept for some time. He reversed himself in double-quick time. He ran back to his mother and said, "Mom, come quickly to the bedroom. There is someone either coming or going right under my bed!"

Our Search for Identity

From about our teens onward we begin to ask, Who am I, really? What am I here for? Where have I come from? Where am I going? These questions surface again and again throughout our lives, particularly in moments of decision or crisis. We ask these questions even more urgently as we move toward death. Our responses to these questions are vital, shaping the way we live, how we relate to each other, and how we interact with the world.

The first gift of struggle is the call to conversion—the call to think differently about who God is and about who I am as an individual. It calls us to think again about what life really means and how I go about being in the world.

—Joan D. Chittister

> *God blesses you exceedingly, for you are God's creature; and God gives you the best of treasures, a vivid intelligence.*
> —Hildegard of Bingen

Some of us look inside to find out who we are. Because we live in a therapeutic culture, this is a popular option today. Of course, it is imperative for us to go on an inner journey. If we don't get to know ourselves, we won't grow into maturity. But we don't find the answer to who we are, exclusively, inside. While the labels we use to describe our inner experiences can often be helpful, we are always more than these labels. Like me, you may be an introvert, but we are always more than that. We are more than our score on the Myers-Briggs Type Indicator, the Enneagram, or whatever personality profile we may use.

Some of us look to others to tell us who we are. Our sense of who we are becomes determined by whatever family or friends say about us. When they applaud and affirm us, we feel like someone of worth and value. But when they don't, we sometimes feel that we are worth little. When we look to others to define who we are, life becomes an emotional roller-coaster ride. Sometimes we are up and sometimes down. It's dangerous to draw our identity solely from what others say about us.

Some of us look to our achievements and to what we own to find out who we are. If we have a lot, drive a good car, own a few status symbols—then we feel like someone special. In a consumer culture that values achievement and success, it's common to derive our sense of identity from things like this. But what happens when we lose these status symbols that we have so carefully accumulated? If we have based our identity on them, how are we going to feel about ourselves?

I recently took in my smallish car for service. The guy at the service station offered to let me drive his car for a day while he worked on mine. So I left my Volkswagen for the day and drove away in his Mercedes-Benz. No one looks at me when I'm in a Volkswagen, but in that Mercedes everyone looked at me. All I needed was some snazzy sunglasses, and I would have been completely swept away. But at the end of the day I had to give back the Mercedes. What would have happened if I had built my identity on it?

Jesus' Source of Identity

In our search for identity Christ meets us right where we are. In his humanity Jesus also needed to know who he was. But he didn't look inward, nor did he let others tell him who he was, nor did he look to his achievements to find his sense of identity. Instead, in order to know who he was, Jesus listened to the voice of his Heavenly Parent, trusted that voice, and claimed its truth for his life.

When Jesus came to John to be baptized, he had already been through thirty years of hidden preparation. Now the moment for him to begin his public ministry was at hand. He went down to the river Jordan and entered the waters. That is one of the most moving moments in the Gospels, when Jesus walks into the water where John baptized sinners. It's a powerful picture of Jesus identifying himself totally and utterly with broken and sinful humanity.

John the Baptizer baptized him, the heavens opened, and Jesus heard a voice from heaven speaking to him. As the Spirit of God descended like a dove on him, he heard the voice say, "This is my Son, the Beloved, with whom I am well pleased" (v. 17). In that moment Jesus entered more deeply into his own identity as the beloved of God. Because he knew who he was, he now was ready to take up the ministry that he had been given.

Jesus heard that voice again later in his life. Remember that moment he came to Jerusalem, when Jesus went up the Mount of Transfiguration (Luke 9:28-35)? There again he heard the same voice saying, "This is my beloved Son" (v. 35, KJV). Just as it had happened at his baptism, Jesus received his identity again from God. Now he was ready to lay down his life, because when God asks you to suffer, you need to know who you are.

> *Within us all there is a yearning that nothing—no thing, no created object, no person, no pleasure—can satisfy. We are athirst for the living God.*
>
> —David Rensberger

Our Belovedness Revealed

Not only is Jesus the beloved of God, he also reveals to us that we too are God's beloved. Have you ever tracked Jesus' interactions with people through the Gospels? He always lets people know that they matter. Whoever they are, whatever they have done, Jesus helps them see that they are God's beloved.

There was a leper living on the margins of society (Mark 1:40-42). Everywhere he went he shouted, "Unclean, unclean." Jesus, moved by compassion, stretched out his hand and touched him. God's love cannot live at arm's length. In that moment the leper knew that he was loved, accepted, and forgiven. He knew that he was beloved of God.

There was a woman caught committing adultery (John 8:1-11). She was surrounded by a group of men ready to stone her for breaking the law of God. In this tense moment Jesus bent down and wrote in the sand. He said to the men, "Let anyone among you who is without sin be the first to throw a stone at her" (v. 7). One by one they walked away, the elders first. Then Jesus turned to the woman and spoke these unforgettable words: "Neither do I condemn you. Go your way, and from now on do not sin again" (v. 11). In that moment the woman knew she was loved, accepted, and forgiven. She knew that she was beloved of God.

There was the despised tax collector Zacchaeus perched in a tree (Luke 19:2-10). Jesus came walking by, looked up, and said to him, "Zacchaeus, hurry and come down; for I must stay at your house today" (v. 5). There was a muttering in the crowd as he went into the house of a known sinner. Can you imagine how Zacchaeus felt as he sat down with Jesus? Loved, accepted, and forgiven. He knew he was beloved of God. Jesus revealed to people that they were infinitely precious, that they mattered, that they were God's beloved.

> *Words are inadequate to describe this loving embrace of God.*
>
> —Michel Quoist

Discovering Our Own Belovedness

Even though Christ reveals to us that we are God's beloved, many of us struggle to believe this good news. We may know it in our heads but not in our hearts. We may have heard other voices throughout our lives telling us we are no good, that we'll never amount to much. Those words sometimes silence any other voices of affirmation. Some of us have been abused. Some of us have been through unspeakable moments of failure, rejection, and suffering. Some of us have been so deeply scarred that we wonder whether anyone really cares about us.

Those of us who struggle to know that we are God's beloved need to hear this: *We discover our belovedness when we come home.* In the story of the prodigal son in Luke 15, the prodigal comes to his senses when he is working with pigs. I have never been impressed by his conversion story. Who wouldn't come to his senses in this situation? In that moment of dereliction he wrote out a repentance speech: "Father, I have sinned against heaven and before you; I am no longer worthy to be called your son; treat me like one of your hired hands" (vv. 18-19). In other words, "Father, after the mess I have made, after the sins I have sinned, after the wrong I have done, I can never hope to be your son again. Just treat me as one of your workers."

The son tucks his speech in his pocket and starts for home. The father has been waiting, longing, looking down that road for months. Then one day he sees a speck in the distance, and he knows it's his son. Love is never blind. What does the father do? He runs down the road, probably holding his robe, his garments fluttering out behind him. What a picture of passionate longing, of reckless love, of heart-felt desire.

When the father meets his son, the boy doesn't even get all the way through his repentance speech. He simply feels the father's arms embrace him. Then come the gifts of the robe and the ring and the sandals. These gifts celebrate who he is. He is the beloved son who belongs to the father. Can you imagine how he felt when he put on that robe of acceptance, that ring of authority, those shoes of belonging? Loved, accepted, forgiven.

Like the prodigal we need to come home, just as we are. "Just as I am, without one plea, but that thy blood was shed for me, . . . O Lamb of God, I come."[1] And as we come home, let us open up our lives more deeply to the Spirit of God. Only the Spirit of God can tell us who we really are. Paul puts it so beautifully: "God has sent the Spirit of his Son into our hearts, crying, 'Abba! Father!'" (Gal. 4:6). The Spirit of God whispers in our depths that we are God's beloved. And then we *know*.

> *When we enter upon the spiritual life, we should consider and examine to the bottom what we are.*
>
> —Brother Lawrence

It's easy to go through the motions of believing without knowing deep down that we are God's beloved. When I came to know Christ at the age of seventeen, I had never been in a church before. Some of my best friends sang in a church group and invited me to join them. Unfortunately, I can't sing, so they switched off the microphone as soon as I started singing. When the group toured around South Africa, I just stood there with a dead microphone. I developed an "up" look for the high notes. On low notes, I crunched up my shoulders. People would say to me afterward, "You've got a magnificent voice." I didn't say anything. I'd just been looking the part, going through the motions.

This story is a parable. So often we go through the motions in our spiritual lives. We sing, we pray, we worship, we give the impression that we know that we are God's beloved. But often in the deep places of our hearts, the assurance is not there; and we know it. We need to come home and let the Spirit of God whisper, "You are God's beloved." I cannot tell you who you are. Others cannot tell you who you are. Only the Spirit of God can.

That happened for me in 1980 during a dark moment in the history of my country, South Africa, and in my life personally. I was working in a city church that was deeply resistant to change. I had my first experience visiting an apartheid jail. I was trying to adjust to the challenges of marriage. I found myself running on empty. I began going through the motions of ministry. In a sad moment I wrote out my letter of resignation as a minister, hoping to go back to work for the tire manufacturing company where I worked before. Then I went on a retreat led by Tom Smail, an Anglican minister from England. He spoke about dry bones and how only the Spirit can give us life. That night I slipped to the floor in a little chapel among my Anglican/Episcopalian brothers and sisters and asked them to pray for me. It was a moment of profound personal vulnerability. Some of them laid their hands on me and prayed that the Spirit of God would descend and bless and fill me.

Nothing much happened at that moment, but when I walked outside, I knew something was different deep inside me. I knew in a new

Layer after layer is removed; and there at the heart, sustaining and nourishing all the other loves, is the love and yearning for God.

—Margaret Guenther

way that I was beloved by God. I had heard the Divine whisper, "Trevor, you are God's beloved." After that, somehow I could go back into the struggle of ministry and do what needed to be done. Many times since that night I've needed to open a little gap in my heart and say again, "Spirit of God, whisper to me and tell me who I am."

If you are unsure about your belovedness, I invite you to listen deeply to the Spirit of God. Listen to the Spirit whisper in your own depths that you are God's beloved. And as you claim your own belovedness, begin to see others also as God's beloved, so that we can participate in our belovedness together. We in the church are not God's elite. God has no favorites. Remember that scripture says, "For God so loved the *world*." Let us begin to see beyond race, beyond culture, beyond gender, beyond sexual orientation, beyond religion, beyond all these externals and see each other as God's beloved. When we relate to others as God relates to us, our sense of being God's beloved deepens even more.

A Closing Story

Roman Catholic theologian Henri Nouwen lectured at some of the top universities in North America. Then he decided to spend the rest of his years working with those with handicapping conditions within the L'Arche movement. In *Life of the Beloved*, he describes a deeply moving moment from the life of his community:

> Not long ago, in my own community, I had a very personal experience of the power of a real blessing. Shortly before I started a prayer service in one of our houses, Janet, a handicapped member of our community, said to me: "Henri can you give me a blessing?" I responded in a somewhat automatic way by tracing with my thumb the sign of the cross on her forehead. Instead of being grateful, however, she protested vehemently, "No, that doesn't work. I want a real blessing!" I suddenly became aware of the ritualistic quality of my response to her request and said, "Oh, I am sorry, . . . let me give you a real blessing when we are all together for the prayer service." She nodded with a smile, and I realized that something special was required of me. After the service, when about thirty people were sitting in a circle on the floor, I said, "Janet has asked me for a special blessing. She feels that she needs that

now." As I was saying this, I didn't know what Janet really wanted. But Janet didn't leave me in doubt for very long. As soon as I said, "Janet has asked me for a special blessing," she stood up and walked toward me. I was wearing a long white robe with ample sleeves covering my hands as well as my arms. Spontaneously, Janet put her arms around me and put her head against my chest. Without thinking, I covered her with my sleeves so that she almost vanished in the folds of my robe. As we held each other, I said, "Janet, I want you to know that you are God's Beloved Daughter. You are precious in God's eyes. Your beautiful smile, your kindness to the people in your house and all the good things you do show us what a beautiful human being you are. I know you feel a little low these days and that there is some sadness in your heart, but I want you to remember who you are: a very special person, deeply loved by God and all the people who are here with you."

As I said these words, Janet raised her head and looked at me; and her broad smile showed that she had really heard and received the blessing. When she returned to her place, Jane, another handicapped woman, raised her hand and said, "I want a blessing too." She stood up and, before I knew it, had put her face against my chest. After I had spoken words of blessing to her, many more of the handicapped people followed, expressing the same desire to be blessed. The most touching moment, however, came when one of the assistants, a twenty-four-year-old student, raised his hand and said, "And what about me?" "Sure," I said. "Come." He came, and, as we stood before each other, I put my arms around him and said, "John, it is so good that you are here. You are God's Beloved Son. Your presence is a joy for all of us. When things are hard and life is burdensome, always remember that you are loved with an everlasting love." As I spoke those words, he looked at me with tears in his eyes and then he said, "Thank you, thank you very much."[2]

We may not be Roman Catholic priests or wear white robes, but we can remind one another that we are God's beloved. We have been formed and created by God in our mothers' wombs. We are known by name. Our names have been carved into the crucified hands of God. We are loved with an everlasting love. There is nothing in all creation, nothing in this world or the next, that can ever separate us from the love of God in Jesus Christ. *Nothing.* When we know that we are God's beloved, we have embarked on the journey toward an authentic Christian spirituality.

DAILY EXERCISES

This week's reading and exercises encourage you to consider for your-self the questions, Who am I, really? What am I here for? Where have I come from? Where am I going? As you reread the story of Jesus' baptism and blessing from God, you will be invited to imagine your-self in the story and to experience God's blessing of belovedness personally. Read Week 1, "Knowing Who We Are," before you begin these reflection exercises. Use your journal to record thoughts and questions as you read the article and then to record responses to these daily exercises. Enter each in a spirit receptive to the presence and calling of Christ and in the knowledge that you are known and beloved by God.

EXERCISE 1   HEARING THE VOICE

In that moment Jesus entered more deeply into his own identity as the beloved of God. Because he knew who he was, he now was ready to take up the ministry that he had been given. (page 21)

Read Matthew 3:13-17. Then read the story again. Enter imagi-natively into Jesus' experience of his baptism. Feel the water. Smell the fresh air. Sense the excitement in the crowd. Explore the ways Jesus may have heard the "voice from heaven." Say verse 17 out loud, placing the emphasis on different words. Which way do you imagine Jesus may have heard it?

Close your eyes and listen again with Jesus to where the "voice from heaven" came from. Did the voice come from outside him or from inside him?

Imagine what the "voice" sounded like—deep like a waterfall, authoritative, soft as a whisper, male, female, loud and declarative, gentle and caring, or something else entirely?

Read the story through a final time in the manner you now hear it. Remain there with Jesus for a minute in a posture of receptivity to God's blessing. Jot down your thoughts and feelings in your journal.

Vocation does not come from willfulness. It comes from listening. I must listen to my life and try to understand what it is truly about . . . or my life will never represent anything real in the world, no matter how earnest my intentions.

—Parker J. Palmer

EXERCISE 2   RECEIVING THE BLESSING

Not only is Jesus the beloved of God, he also reveals to us that we too are God's beloved. (page 21)

Read Matthew 3:13-17. Notice that in Matthew's version of Jesus' baptism, we read that a voice from heaven said, "This is my Son…," whereas in Mark's version, the voice said, "You are my Son…" (Mark 1:11). What do you make of the difference in these two versions of the experience?

Write in your journal a paraphrase of the blessing that Jesus heard and received in Matthew 3:17. Feel free to improvise.

Now close your eyes and listen for where you may have heard (or felt) a similar blessing through persons or experiences that have graced your life. As memories surface, pause and savor them; listen afresh to the voice that still sounds through them. Note these memories in your journal.

If no such memory surfaces, then reread your paraphrase of the blessing Jesus heard and receive it for yourself as a blessing that God wants you to hear through Christ.

EXERCISE 3   SEEING OURSELVES THROUGH GOD'S EYES

Our responses to these questions … shape the way we live, how we relate to each other, and how we interact with the world. (page 19)

Read Matthew 3:13-17. While we hope that God's voice will be clear and central, many voices and experiences help define who we are and how we understand ourselves. To consider the many shaping forces in your life, divide a page (or pages) in your journal into four sections and write one of the following four questions at the top of each section: Who am I, really? What am I here for? Where have I come from? Where am I going?

Spend a few moments responding to each question—not long essays but your first impressions and immediate thoughts. When each question has been addressed briefly, step back and see what this snapshot of yourself tells you. How do your responses to the questions shape the way that you live and relate to others?

Pray, asking God's wisdom and guidance to see yourself both honestly and lovingly, from God's perspective, as a beloved child. Write your prayer in your journal.

EXERCISE 4   SEEING OTHERS AS GOD'S BELOVED

As you claim your own belovedness, begin to see others also as God's beloved, so that we can participate in our belovedness together. (page 25)

Read Matthew 3:13-17. Experiment today with treating those you meet as God's beloved. Begin with a practice of beholding each person for whom he or she really is in God. It may help to carry verse 17 (or your paraphrase) with you in your mind and heart as a reminder. Then let the Spirit lead you as you seek to relate to them as God's beloved in any number of ways: acknowledging their presence in a special way, greeting them warmly, taking a special interest in their lives, listening to them with genuine interest and anticipation, reaching out with little acts of helpfulness, or receiving them in a posture of courtesy and respect.

Take a moment to prepare inwardly by meditating on the blessing in verse 17, as persons you are likely to encounter today come to mind. Imagine beholding each one as God's beloved.

At the end of the day record the results of your experiment. How did you see and relate to people differently? How did they respond? What did you find most difficult?

Talk with God about the day's experiment. Ask for grace to see each person even more clearly for who she or he is to God. Lift each to God in thanksgiving.

EXERCISE 5   REMEMBERING WHO WE ARE

We have been formed and created by God in our mothers' wombs. We are known by name. (page 26)

Read Matthew 3:13-17. Throughout the Bible many passages underscore the fact of our belovedness to God. Search the scriptures and identify the most meaningful passages that say something significant about the way God sees and values you. Draw on your favorite translations. Below is a list of some familiar verses to help you get started.

As you read and reflect on the list you have made, write in your journal the phrases from those verses that most speak to you, words that express what the "voice from heaven" says to you and what you need to remember.

Spend five minutes in silence, pondering what you have written and abiding in the love that God extends to you through Jesus Christ.

Psalm 139
Isaiah 42:1-4
Isaiah 43:1-7
Matthew 3:13-17
Mark 1:9-11
Luke 15:1-7, 8-10, 11-32
Ephesians 1:3-14

Remember to review the insights recorded in your notebook or journal for the week in preparation for the group meeting.

Changing from the Inside

Read Mark 1:14-20

A young Catholic priest prepared seven years for ordination. Eventually the day arrived when he could celebrate the Eucharist for the first time. In the Catholic liturgy the priest begins by saying, "May the peace of the Lord be with you." And the people respond, "And also with you." That day the service was packed with family, friends, bishops, and congregation members. When the young priest came to the podium to begin the service, he found his microphone wasn't working. So he said to the congregation, "There is something wrong with this mike." And the people responded, "And also with you."

That story is a parable of the relationship between the church and world. We look out at the world around us and say, "There is something wrong with you." And they say in response, "And also with you."

A friend who has been a clinical psychologist for thirty years recently said, "When it comes to people's responses to crises, I see very little difference between those who have grown up in church congregations and those who haven't." So we say to the world, "There is something wrong with you." And the world says to us, "And also with you."

Over the past few years we South Africans have experienced the wonder of being a democracy. The journey into democracy also has had its dark side. There has been a frightening upsurge in violent crime. Recently our neighbor was shot dead in his driveway—for his

> *Courage does not come in a burst of insight. Courage comes out of the way we think and the way we live from Sunday to Sunday, every week of our lives.*
>
> —Joan D. Chittister

car, a 1978 Opel. South Africa has one of the highest child sexual exploitation rates in the world.[1] Statistics tell us that a woman is raped there every seven seconds. In 2003 a number of church leaders visited President Thabo Mbeki to speak about the situation in the country. One of the government officials stood to address the church leaders. "When we came into power as the African National Congress government, we promised you a new constitution and we delivered one of the best constitutions in the world," he said. "You promised us people with new hearts. Where are they?"

So the church says to the world, "There is something wrong with you." And the world says to the church, "And also with you."

Perhaps that is why the atheist philosopher Friedrich Nietzsche purportedly said, "I cannot believe in your savior until the disciples look more saved."

Mahatma Gandhi was deeply attracted to the person of Jesus but never actually moved into Christian community. I wonder if his hesitancy had to do with his experience as a young lawyer in the atmosphere of white rule and ascendancy in South African culture, including its churches. "How could he really see Christ through all this racialism," wrote his friend E. Stanley Jones.[2]

So the church says to the world, "There's something wrong with you." And the world says in response, "And also with you."

We already have said that a crucial ingredient of authentic Christian spirituality is a deep assurance of our belovedness. Another ingredient is an experience of authentic transforming discipleship. What does this involve for you and me?

Jesus is a challenger, a mentor, and provocateur. Each of his challenges invites us into creative conflict with ourselves, stirring the latent capacities of our souls into bud, blossom, and growing fruit.

—Robert C. Morris

The Gospel according to Jesus

In Jesus' first sermon in Mark 1:14-20 he says to the disciples, "I've got good news for you: the kingdom of God is at hand." He seems to say most simply that God is accessible and available to everyone. We are able to live with God in God's kingdom even now. Can you imagine what this good news meant for people in Jesus' time? They repeatedly had been told that only certain people were acceptable to God. Now they were hearing that God was accepting ordinary men and women into the kingdom, no matter who they were or where they were from. This was the gospel that Jesus preached.

Unfortunately, some of us grew up hearing a different gospel. The gospel I first heard went something like this: "Come to Jesus, get your sins forgiven, and get ready to go to heaven." Please don't misunderstand me. Getting our sins forgiven so that we can go to heaven is essential. But this is not the whole gospel that Jesus preached. His gospel is that life in the kingdom of God is now available, that we can live with God in the here and now and discover in God's presence a radical new way of life. The gospel is not about getting into heaven so much as it is about getting heaven into us before we die. Richard Rohr wrote, "It's heaven all the way to heaven. And it's hell all the way to hell."[3] The gospel is about living a new way of life with God in our world today.

Notice also in this passage from Mark the call to discipleship. In Mark 1:17 Jesus says, "Follow me and I will make you fish for people." On one hand, Jesus affirms the availability of the kingdom to everyone. On the other hand, Jesus calls men and women into a journey of transforming discipleship. Both go together. And what God has joined together, let no person put asunder.

We cannot experience the reality of the kingdom without becoming disciples. Jesus is clear. The way to know the reality of God's power and presence is through transforming discipleship. Without discipleship there is no experience of the kingdom in the way that Jesus would want us to know it. Are you on the journey of transforming discipleship? Here are some markers to know that you are on the way. These four markers all come from that explosive little verse, "Follow me and I will make you fish for people."

Each of us has boundaries in our lives that we may hesitate to cross. . . . They may be external and visible borders, or invisible and interior. In any case, justice requires us to cross those thresholds that separate us from the poor, the sick, the friendless, the needy— to follow Jesus.
—Deborah Smith Douglas

Jesus Is the One

We are on the way of transforming discipleship when, first, *we allow Jesus Christ to be the ultimate point of reference for our lives.* Jesus says, "Follow me." In other words, he asks us to become his students, his learners, his apprentices. He becomes our mentor. This is where the journey really begins, when we say to Jesus, "You are the one that I want to love and to follow."

Sometimes I think we make Jesus too small. Jesus is not small. Jesus is big. Yes, he was a little baby born in Bethlehem, but he's more than that! He was a preacher and a healer, but he's more than that. He was the Savior nailed to the cross whispering forgiveness to the world, but he's more than that. He is the one risen from the grave; the conqueror over sin, death, and evil; but he's even more than that. In the magnificent words of Paul, he is the image of the invisible God, the one through whom all things were made and in whom everything holds together (Col. 1:15–17). When we are overwhelmed by this vision of Jesus, our response can only be "Jesus, you are the one I want to love and follow."

My friend Dallas Willard is a professor in a secular university. One day one of his philosophy Ph.D. students said to him, "Dallas, you are a smart man. Why do you follow Jesus?" Dallas, being a good philosopher, answered the question with a question: "Tell me, who else do you have in mind?"

Indeed, who else is worthy of being followed? Adam Smith? Karl Marx? Sigmund Freud? Oprah? Dr. Phil? Who else is there? Jesus is the one. When we believe Jesus to be the one, we want to give ourselves wholeheartedly to him. We want to spend the rest of our lives learning from him how to live our own lives as Jesus would if he were in our place. We want to be with him so that we can become like him.

> *It is life moving Godward, life lived into God's inviting mystery. And because God receives us, takes us, spins us around, and aims us ever outward, life for another invariably focuses us on others.*
>
> —Sue Monk Kidd

Jesus Comes with Friends

The second marker of the journey of transforming discipleship is that *we open our lives to the friends of Jesus*. Go back to Mark 1:14-20. Recall how Jesus called Andrew and Simon Peter, then James and John. As they responded to Jesus individually, before they knew it, they were bound together with one another.

It's always like that. When you open your life to Jesus, he never comes alone. When we open our hearts to Jesus, he comes with his arms around his brothers and sisters. Some are black, and some are white. Some are rich, and some are poor. Some are male, and some are female. Some are gay, and some are straight. He brings them all into my life. I can't say, "Jesus, I want you but not your family."

Jesus is the head of his body. We always want to work out who's in, who's out, who's up, who's down, but that's not our business. I can't say, "I don't like Mr. So-and-So, and he should go join another church." Jesus says, "If you want me, you are stuck with my family. Work it out together."

Consider the first group of disciples. Simon the Zealot was filled with hatred toward the Romans. On the other hand, Matthew was the tax collector for the Romans. Perhaps Simon the Zealot came to Jesus when Matthew was not around and said, "Jesus, why do you hang out with Matthew? He's a sellout." And I imagine Matthew said, "Jesus, do you know what Simon the Zealot's been up to?" Jesus probably said to both of them, "If you want to be with me, work it out." This is transforming discipleship. We open our lives to Jesus, and he brings his friends. There are no private salvation deals available. It's never just me and Jesus.

Changed from the Inside Out

The third marker of the journey is this: When we open our lives to Jesus and his friends, *he changes us inwardly.* He says, "Come with me, and I will reshape you, recreate you, reform you." Jesus accepts us as we are but never leaves us as we are. As we open up to him, he begins a transforming work in our lives from the inside out, forming his heart in our heart, his mind in our mind. The love that woos us, the love that draws us, also changes us. But we don't sit back and do nothing. Although grace is opposed to earning, grace is not opposed to effort. If we want to experience the change that Jesus can bring, we need to cooperate with him.

We cooperate with Jesus through practicing spiritual disciplines such as prayer, Bible reading, fasting, and service. Yet the deepest way we can open our lives to the transforming love of Jesus Christ is to stop

The incarnation of God in human flesh is the defining mystery of Christian life and faith, wherein God and humanity, two spheres of existence, meet in wondrous exchange.

—Michael Downey

pretending and become honest about who we are. As the hymn says, "Just as I am, without one plea, . . . O Lamb of God, I come."[4] Just as I am—warts and all.

Anthony de Mello, the Jesuit Indian priest, told the story of a man who went to the doctor with a splitting headache. The doctor asked him, "Do you smoke a bit?"

"No," he answered, "not at all."

"Well then," the doctor continued, "do you drink a bit?"

"No," the man answered, "I never touch the stuff."

"Do you mess around with women?" the doctor asked.

"No, I would never dream of such a thing," the man said.

The doctor then asked the man, "Is it a sharp, shooting pain you are feeling?"

"Why, yes," said the man.

"It's your halo," the doctor replied. "It's on too tight."[5]

The heart of pretense is trying to look better than we really are. When we take off our halos and come as we are, honestly, something begins to happen in our lives.

The levels of duplicity, darkness, and pretense in our lives are deep. I caught myself the other day in just such a situation. A man from my church congregation called me to say, "Your sermon this morning touched me deeply." Wanting to come across as very caring, I replied, "It was so good to see you this morning at worship." Now I hadn't really seen him, but I assumed that he had been there. He said, "Trevor, I wasn't there. Someone dropped a tape of your sermon at my home immediately after the service." Jesus, have mercy on me! I've been following Jesus for thirty-seven years, and I still am pretending to be who I'm not.

If we want to go on a journey of transformation, we need to get honest. We take off our halos and say, "God, I need you. I bring my prejudice before you, my racism. I bring my addictions, my greed, my need to have more. I bring my fear of not living up to others' expectations that keeps me stuck in pretense." We bring it all before Jesus and ask him to heal us, liberate us, transform us. We can never shock God. And the more honest we are, the deeper our experience of God's love. "Just as I am, without one plea."

The heart allows us to enter into relationships and become sons and daughters of God and brothers and sisters of each other.

—Henri J. M. Nouwen

A Heart for People

The final marker is this: We are on the journey of transforming discipleship when *what we value most in life is people.* "Follow me," says Jesus, "and I will make you fish for people." For years I didn't like this passage. I couldn't understand that Jesus wanted me to go and catch people.

Then about fourteen years ago a fisherman named Mark said to me, "I want to teach you to catch fish." "I'm game," I said. He came around at half past four on a Monday morning. At half past five, we were sitting in the dark alongside the Vaal River, cleaning bait. By six A.M. in the pitch dark we were sitting on the lake. I was thinking to myself, *this man is passionate about fishing.*

Suddenly this verse in Mark's Gospel came alive for me. Jesus is speaking to fishermen. He knows where their passion lies—with fish. Jesus says, "Come with me, and I will give you a new heart. I will replace your passion for fish with a passion for people. I will give you a new love for people so that every human being becomes valuable to you." The acid test of being on a journey of transforming discipleship is whether people are becoming more and more important to us. Are our lives filled with new respect, reverence, and courtesy for people, whoever they may be?

Desmond Tutu, a former South African archbishop, was first attracted to the Christian faith when he was a nine-year-old growing up in a township, a disadvantaged area outside one of our South African cities. There was a white Anglican priest working among black people in that township. This was in the 1940s, during the terrible days of apartheid. Tutu's mother was a maid. One day Tutu saw that priest, Trevor Huddleston, walk past his mother, a black domestic worker, and lift his hat in greeting. In that moment, Tutu knew there must be something to the Christian faith.[6]

There are two movements that must be plainly present in every complete spiritual life. The energy of its prayer must be directed on the one hand towards God; and on the other toward people.

—Evelyn Underhill

Conclusion

Are you on the journey of transforming discipleship? Keep these four markers before you: (1)We see Jesus as the one. (2) We open our lives to the friends of Jesus. (3) We embark on a journey of deep change, honesty, and transparency. And, (4) we allow Jesus to form in us a heart for people.

This is the journey that will lead us into the reality of the kingdom. Remember always that we cannot have one without the other. We will experience life with God more deeply and more intimately when we follow Jesus along the road of transforming discipleship. And as we embark on this journey, Jesus steps out of the Gospels and becomes for us our living and ever-present companion and mentor, our Lord and Friend. We will never be alone.

DAILY EXERCISES

"Follow me and I will make you fish for people." This vision of discipleship has been taken up by followers of Jesus in every generation since the beginning of his ministry. This week's reading and exercises explore Jesus' vision in terms of what it means for our self-understanding, our relationships, and our lives in Christ. Read Week 2, "Changing from the Inside," before working through the following exercises this week. Record in your journal the thoughts, feelings, ideas, and questions that arise as you read the article and complete the daily exercises. Begin your exercises each day by taking a moment to center yourself in openness to God.

EXERCISE 1   PRACTICING AWARENESS OF GOD'S AVAILABILITY

The gospel is about living a new way of life with God. (page 33)

Read Mark 1:14-15. After you have read these verses, close your eyes and imagine you are there when Jesus launches his ministry. What is the "good news" for the people when Jesus says, "The kingdom of God has come near?" What difference does this make to those who are listening?

Reflect on what the nearness of God's reign means for you. How near is it?

To repent is to turn away from something in order to turn toward God. Today, practice turning your awareness toward God; practice an awareness of God's nearness and availability in all times and circumstances, to yourself and to all. Choose one of the following ideas, or one of your own, to help you practice your awareness of God today:

- Meditate on the Revised Standard Version translation of Mark 1:15: "The kingdom of God is at hand." As you touch people and things today, remember God working with you and through your hands.

- Place a symbol of God's presence—a cross, stone, or picture—in your pocket or on your desk, so that you can stop and touch it several times today as a reminder to be in touch with God.

- Set your watch or other alarm to go off as a reminder to pause and observe certain times of prayer throughout the day.

Keep a record of your experience in your journal.

EXERCISE 2   ACCEPTING JESUS CHRIST AS OUR MENTOR

We are on the way of transforming discipleship when . . . we allow Jesus Christ to be the ultimate point of reference for our lives. (page 33)

Read Mark 1:16-20. By responding to Jesus' call, these four new disciples look to Jesus as their mentor in how to live with God in the world. What words and phrases in the story stand out for you? What do you find exciting and scary about this picture of transforming discipleship?

Spend a few moments listening to the call and promise in Jesus' words, "Follow me and I will make you fish for people." Imagine him speaking as directly to you as he spoke to those on the shore of the Sea of Galilee. In all honesty, what voices in you respond "yes," "no," or "I'm not sure"? Use your journal to capture your inner dialogue.

Now respond to Jesus in prayer as directly as he is addressing you. If it helps, pull up an empty chair and imagine him sitting before you. Tell him heart to heart your feelings about having him as your lifelong mentor. How has his mentoring already impacted your life? Sense Jesus' response and engage in prayerful conversation.

Give thanks to God for whatever Jesus may be inviting you to receive and to do at this point.

EXERCISE 3   RECEIVING JESUS' FRIENDS

The second marker of the journey of transforming discipleship is that we open our lives to the friends of Jesus. (page 34)

Read Mark 1:16-20. The story shows how Jesus began to create a new kind of family made up of people seeking to live in step with him. Imagine the changes that must have taken place in how the followers of Jesus related to one another. What do you think were their greatest challenges?

Scan the membership of those who make up your community of faith. Make three lists:

- First, list those with whom you would probably be family or friends under any circumstances.
- Second, list those you would probably never know or associate with except for your common friendship with Jesus Christ.
- Third, list those people (or kinds of people) you still have great difficulty accepting as part of the community of Jesus' disciples or maybe even as children of God.

In prayer, share your third list with your spiritual mentor, Jesus Christ. Go through the list name by name; admit your feelings about each one, then pause to listen to Christ. What might he be calling you to say, do, or be in relation to the people on your third list? Ask him if there is any specific action that will affirm your family identity with this person or these people. Make a plan for acting on what you hear, and write it in your journal. Close by lifting each person to God and by opening yourself to the Spirit's guidance.

EXERCISE 4 CHANGING FROM THE INSIDE OUT: STOP PRETENDING

The deepest way we can open our lives to the transforming love of Jesus Christ is to stop pretending and become honest about who we are. . . . warts and all. (pages 35–36)

Read Mark 1:16-20. Mark writes that these disciples "left their nets and followed him." As disciples we are challenged to leave behind another aspect of our outer selves: our pretense. "When we take off our halos and come as we are, honestly, something begins to happen in our lives" (page 36).

What are some of the "halos" you wear?

What would it mean to take off some of these halos in the presence of Jesus and one another? In a moment of quiet prayer, see what it's like to come before Jesus without any pretense. Imagine coming just as you are. How do you experience Jesus in this moment of self-disclosure? Do you still experience yourself as God's beloved?

Make notes on your experience in your journal.

EXERCISE 5   DEEPENING YOUR PASSION FOR PEOPLE

We are on the journey of transforming discipleship when what we value most in life is people. (page 37)

Read Mark 1:16-20. Jesus' words in verse 17 ("Follow me and I will make you fish for people") contain promise as well as command—the promise of being mentored by Jesus, becoming someone like him, and maturing in God's passionate love for people. Ponder the promise of having in you a passion for people as strong as a fisherman's passion for fishing.

Is this a passion you desire? What would an all-consuming passion for people displace in your life?

Imagine that Jesus is awaiting a response from you, a response to his call, "Follow me and I will make you fish for people." Write a letter to him in response. Tell him your yes's, your no's, your questions, and your wrestling.

Sit quietly with what you have written. Remember that Jesus Christ is near, and listen to his response in your heart. Record what you hear.

Remember to review the insights recorded in your notebook or journal for the week in preparation for the group meeting.

Listening to the Groans

Read Romans 8:22-27

Have you heard the story of the three tourists who visited South Africa? On their last night in Johannesburg, they went out for a night on the town and decided to paint the town red. When they got back to the hotel, they were really under the weather. They were wobbly on their feet and slurred in speech.

To make matters worse, there had been a power outage, which often happens in Johannesburg; and the hotel had been plunged into darkness. The tourists' room was on the sixtieth floor, and the elevators weren't working. To make the ordeal of climbing the stairs to their room a bit easier, they decided to tell stories on the way up. For the first twenty floors one would tell funny stories. For the next twenty floors another would tell ghost stories. And for the last twenty floors the third one would tell sad stories.

Off they went, climbing and tripping up the stairs, telling stories all the while. As they climbed the first twenty floors, they laughed at the funny stories. They heard ghost stories for the next twenty floors and were scared out of their wits. When it came time for the sad stories, the third guy didn't say a word.

Eventually, after three and a half hours of climbing, they reached the sixtieth floor. Intrigued by the third guy's silence, the other two said to him, "You were supposed to tell us sad stories, but you said nothing." He said, "You know, guys, I don't know how to say this, but I forgot to pick up the key for our room at the reception desk."

The spirituality of struggle is a process. It is, too, a catalyst and a series of gifts without which we cannot possibly become fully ourselves.

—Joan D. Chittister

The Key of Listening

That story can be a parable for us. It is tragic for us to get to the sixtieth floor and suddenly realize that we haven't got the key to an authentic spirituality. Listening is that key and the basis for all Christian ministry and mission. It's the key to healing, evangelism, pastoral care, community building, and peacemaking. It links the inward and outward journeys. It saves us from a false inwardness. Listening helps us to love God with all our heart, soul, mind, and strength. It helps us to love our neighbors even as we seek to love ourselves. Listening can help us in all these ways.

The Annunciation is an unforgettable painting by Philippe de Champaigne that portrays Mary's being impregnated through her hearing (see back flap of this book). In the image, as the angel appears to her, a shaft of light comes into her ear, and the Holy Spirit is in the light. We all need to open our ears to be impregnated by the Spirit, so that with Mary we can bear Christ into the world.

During World War II theologian Dietrich Bonhoeffer was one of the few German Christians who resisted the tyranny of Hitler. In the midst of that national trauma, he helped build a confessing church.[1] As a young adult I feasted on his books *The Cost of Discipleship* and *Letters and Papers from Prison*. Those books were manna for me at that time in South Africa's history. In another book called *Life Together*, written over sixty years ago, Bonhoeffer wrote these words: "Many people are looking for an ear that will listen. They do not find it among Christians, because these Christians are talking where they should be listening."[2] He goes on to say that Christians who have stopped listening to their neighbor will soon stop listening to God as well.

That is why before we get to the sixtieth floor, we need to pick up this key of listening. To get a sense of what listening is like, read Paul's words in Romans 8. All the rich, deep themes of an authentic Christian spirituality are found in this chapter. In verses 22–27, Paul refers to three groans to which all followers of Jesus need to listen. As we listen to these different groans, we build a bridge between the inner journey and the outer journey. Additionally, we find ourselves being deliv-

Once we have truly struggled with something that stretches the elastic of the spirit, we are worthy to walk with others in struggle, too. Then we're ready to listen.

—Joan D. Chittister

ered from a private spirituality. As we listen to the groans we also find ourselves able to love God with all our hearts, souls, minds, and strength, and our neighbors as ourselves.

Creation Groans

First of all, we need to listen to *the groans of all of creation.* In verse 22 Paul writes, "We know that the whole creation has been groaning in labor pains until now." Although much can be said regarding the groans of the wider creation, Paul invites us to pay attention to the groans of people, of human creation around us. Sometimes the more "spiritual" we become, the less attention we pay to the cries of the world. I remember how I used to sing these words as a part of the song "I Have Decided to Follow Jesus": "The world behind me, the cross before me."[3] Yet, the cross is *in* the world. The crucifixion of Jesus, his passion, is not only on the movie screen; it's in the world and before our eyes and in our ears—every day of our lives.

Another song I sang went like this: "Turn your eyes upon Jesus, look full in his wonderful face, and the things of earth will grow strangely dim."[4] Although I understand what the songwriter meant by this, I believe the things of earth will grow strangely *clear* in the light of Jesus' glory and grace. He is the light of the world so that we can see it more clearly and hear it more deeply. When we open our lives to Jesus, he draws us more deeply into the world that he loved and for which he died.

If God reads *Time* magazine, I think God reads the religion section last. God loves the world; the world is God's first love. And because God wants to mend the world, we are called into the world to hear its groans. When we listen to the groans, we get a glimpse of what it may mean to follow Jesus more faithfully in the world in which we live.

In the early eighties, South Africa was a desperate place to live. Although our country was in a state of emergency, my predominately white congregation and I lived in a little bubble, as Peter Storey calls it. In this little bubble we went to school, raised our families, and went to church. When we entertained tourists from overseas, they thought

> *Both humans and nature await redemption through Christ. Nature, like humanity, is a victim of transience and death. . . . The natural world with autumnal melancholy . . . [yearns] for release from bondage, which it suffers but did not cause.*
>
> —Frederick Quinn

we were very nice, that we were good, decent, and hospitable people. But the great tragedy was that we let our institutions do our sinning for us. In our little bubble we were deeply disconnected from the groans of the majority of people who lived in our midst.

I remember returning to Johannesburg from Soweto where I had taken a group of overseas visitors. As I was driving back, some words appeared on the screen of my mind: "Trevor, take members of your congregation into those areas where their brothers and sisters suffer." It was that clear. So, for the next fifteen years or more, I went with groups of people from the congregation on pilgrimages of pain and hope in our own country. We were getting outside the bubble. We did not go as tourists but as pilgrims. We went to listen to the groans. Over the years I watched people change as they listened. Jesus came in that light as it entered their ears, and they were impregnated by the Spirit.

Maybe we can't all go on eight-day pilgrimages, but we can develop a way of life that listens to the groans of those outside our bubble. It will save us from a life of faith that cuts itself off from the world that God loves so much. This happened for Evelyn Underhill, that wonderful modern-era Christian mystic. There was a time in her life when she nearly went down a very private spiritual path. But she had a discerning spiritual director, Baron Friedrich von Hügel, who wrote her a letter as if he could read her heart. He asked Evelyn to spend one hour a week with those who suffer deeply. And as Evelyn did that, she heard the groans. Jesus began to unite in her the inner and outer journey and saved her from a false inwardness.[5]

If we knew how to listen to God, if we knew how to look around us, our whole life would become prayer.

—Michel Quoist

We Groan

We also need to *listen to our own deep groans*. We find this dimension of listening in verse 23. "Not only the creation," says Paul, "but we ourselves, who have the first fruits of the Spirit, groan inwardly while we wait for adoption, the redemption of our bodies." Here Paul magnificently describes the tension in which we all live. On one hand, we experience the first fruits of the Spirit. We know the joy of being God's beloved, of having our sins forgiven, of being reconciled with God. We have God's Holy Spirit living within us, testifying with our own spirit that we are sons and daughters. We know that we are loved, accepted, and forgiven. But then Paul also says we—you and I—groan inwardly.

In 1978 I worked for eight weeks with Gordon Cosby at the Church of the Saviour in Washington, D.C. The day before I came back to South Africa, Gordon and I were having coffee together, and I asked him a question I ask people I respect: "If you could say one thing to me, what would it be?" He was quiet for a moment and then he said, "When you go back to South Africa, always remember that every one of the people you pastor sits next to his or her own pool of tears."

I've never forgotten this image. It's an awareness with which I constantly live. Each time I speak or teach or simply am with people, I'm aware of the pool of tears that each of us sits next to. To become aware of the inward groans of others, begin by listening to your own groans. Befriend your own pain; don't run from it. Addictions result from covering up or running from pain. We do anything to keep the pain away and then wonder why we feel so dead.

Whatever is in your pool of tears, befriend it. Find a wailing wall, and let your pain find its voice. God calls us to attend to our pain. Often it is there that we find the seeds of our own calling in the world. We see this so often around us. The recovering alcoholic reaches out to another alcoholic. The person who has lost a child reaches out compassionately to another parent who has lost a child. Parents of a mentally handicapped child reach out to others who have this experience. Through our own pain God speaks and often gives a sense for what God wants us to be about in this world.

Our suffering offers us an opportunity to grow, to change, and to be spiritually transformed through it. This will not happen, however, unless we meet our pain in a compassionate way and willingly spend time with it.

—Joyce Rupp

The Spirit Groans

We must also listen to the groans of God. In verse 26 we read, "Likewise the Spirit helps us in our weakness; for we do not know how to pray as we ought." We don't know what we ought to pray for, but the Spirit intercedes for us with groans that words cannot express. It's not only creation that groans; it's not only we who groan; it is also the Spirit of God who groans in us. We worship a God who groans.

I talk a lot about our picture of God. It is one of the most fundamental issues in our faith. Who is the God we worship? What is our God like? This question is critical because we become like the God we worship. Our lives are expressed in part according to our pictures of God.

Paul introduces us to a God who groans. We are tempted to think God is far away, aloof, distant. Bette Midler sings, "God is watching us from a distance."[6] But that song is wrong. Jesus, who is the image of the invisible God, gives us a different picture. Jesus' weeping with Mary and Martha as they grieve reminds us that God weeps too. When Jesus cries out, "My God, my God, why have you forsaken me?" he reminds us that God enters into our pain and our forsakenness. Even beyond crucifixion, in his resurrection body in heaven, Jesus bears the scars. We worship a God who grieves, who weeps, who groans with us and all humanity.

Amazingly, we can relieve God's suffering in God's people. From his prison cell, Dietrich Bonhoeffer wrote: "Christians stand by God in his hour of grieving."[7] This is God's hour of grieving. The passion of Jesus continues in the world 'round about us. And when we hear the groans of God in the suffering of God's people, we are pulled into a radical discipleship and a robust faith that leads us to love God and love people.

But the groan of the Spirit is also a groan of intercession. The Spirit is praying, inside of me, inside of you. The Spirit of God takes the intercession of Jesus before the Father in heaven and all the time prays it within our hearts. There is a prayer meeting constantly going on in our lives. We are never prayerless. The Spirit intercedes deep within us, praying the prayer of Jesus, that we may be one and that this world will be mended.

But how do we embrace the beauty of this world and listen to the groans at the same time? We look to people like Dorothy Day, Jean Vanier, Mother Teresa, and Desmond Tutu. What strikes me about these people who have lived so deeply with those who suffer is their

Deep speaks to deep, spirit speaks to spirit, heart speaks to heart. I started to realize that there was a mutuality of love not based on shared knowledge or shared feelings, but on shared humanity.

—Henri J. M. Nouwen

joy, a bright radiance and light in them. As they listened to the groans, the light came into their ears, and Jesus came in and filled them with a wild joy. May it be so with us also.

Prayer

God, we know that you are a joyful being. We know that as you embrace the beauty of this world, in your joyful heart there is a place of deep suffering. We want to stand with you. God, give us the gift of ears so we can hear the groan of creation in all its vastness, of the trees and of the rivers, of the mountains and of the air. The groans of the animals that you have given us and the groans of our brothers and of our sisters outside our little bubble. Give us ears to hear and to listen. Lord, give us the courage to face our own pain. We all sit next to our pool of tears, broken relationships, addictions, darknesses that don't seem to go away, an aching loneliness, a deep grief. And sometimes, when our mouth is wide with song, people do not know that we cry. Help us, Lord, to befriend our own pain and to know that in that place you meet us, to weep and grieve with us. Help us somehow to live beyond our pain. Call us forth, Loving God, and may our pain become a gift that we offer to others. Lord, we want to hear your intercession. We thank you that you are praying for us. Even in those moments that we seem prayerless, we are never prayerless, because you are always at prayer within us. Help us to hear your deep intercession for this world and give us the faith and the courage to respond. In the name of Jesus, our Lord, whom we love so deeply. Amen.

DAILY EXERCISES

Listening to the groans of all creation (especially of humanity) of our own hearts, and of God's Spirit, is crucial to an authentic Christian spirituality. This week's reading and exercises invite you to engage in deep listening to both the deep woundedness and profound hope that run like currents through all the hidden and open spaces of the world. Read Week 3, "Listening to the Groans," before working through the following exercises this week. As you read and complete the daily exercises, take time to note your thoughts, feelings, ideas, and questions in your journal. Practice your listening skills as you read the recommended scriptures, as you encounter people each day, and as you discern God's movement in and through creation.

EXERCISE 1   LISTENING TO THE GROANING OF CREATION

As we listen to these different groans, we build a bridge between the inner journey and the outer journey. . . . we also find ourselves able to love God with all our hearts, souls, minds, and strength, and our neighbors as ourselves. (pages 44–45)

Where is this peace to be found? The answer is clear. In weakness. First of all, in our own weakness, in those places of our hearts where we feel most broken, most insecure, most in agony, most afraid.

—Henri J. M. Nouwen

Read Romans 8:22. We want to respond this week in concrete ways to Paul's invitation to pay attention to the "whole creation"—people, earth, and the world around us—"groaning in labor pains until now," waiting for the new creation.

Take yourself on a journey of holy imagination around the globe. See yourself circling the earth and listening carefully to the cries of creation. Move slowly past the places of pain and suffering that are wrapped in poverty, disease, heartache, and grief. Where would you like to touch down on your world tour and immerse yourself? Tune your ears to hear the variety of hurts felt by humanity and the created order in that place. Make a list in your journal of what you have seen on your journey.

Pray that God will help you to be open to hearing the groans of creation and will spark your imagination with ways to respond lovingly.

EXERCISE 2   LISTENING TO THE GROANING WITHIN US

To become aware of the inward groans of others, begin by listening to your own groans. (page 47)

Read Romans 8:22-23. In the article, Trevor Hudson reminds us that everyone "sits next to his or her own pool of tears." What pain, grief, and suffering has filled your pool of tears? What are the groans rising from that pool? Write your thoughts in your journal.

Paul's words in Romans 8 also suggest that our groaning arises from waiting in hope. Reflect in your journal on the hope for which you wait and work. What is the promise or possibility for which you yearn as you groan inwardly?

Finally, allow the Spirit to bring to mind other people that your own deep suffering and hope connect you to. In your journal reflect on your connection with others and with Christ.

To close your prayer time, sit quietly and get in touch with the groaning within you that is deeper than words. Offer it up to God, not in words but in the language of feelings—deep sighs, humming, or song.

EXERCISE 3   LISTENING TO THE GROANING OF GOD

We worship a God who grieves, who weeps, who groans with us and all humanity. (page 48)

Read Romans 8:26-27. Reflect on Dietrich Bonhoeffer's statement: "Christians stand by God in his hour of grieving." Think about an issue that currently dominates the news. Where in this situation does God grieve and groan? Make some notes in your journal about what you see in the news and what you hear in your heart.

Hearing the groaning and grief of God is an invitation to "radical discipleship and a robust faith that leads us to love God and love people." Close your eyes and stay in touch with God's groans, interceding with "sighs too deep for words." What we say to someone in deep grief is not nearly as important as our loving presence. Focus for a time on simply being present with God in the suffering of the world.

How is the Spirit calling you to stand with God in the midst of human need? Write your insights in your journal.

EXERCISE 4   THE CHALLENGE OF LISTENING

Listening is . . . the basis for all Christian ministry and mission. . . . It links the inward and outward journeys. It saves us from a false inwardness. (page 44)

TRANSFIGURATION Read Matthew 17:1-8. In the midst of the outward journey toward Jerusalem, three disciples experience Jesus for who he really is during a time of prayer. "From the cloud a voice says, 'This is my Son, the Beloved; with him I am well pleased; *listen to him!*'" (v. 5, emphasis added).

Reflect on the place and quality of listening in your walk with Christ. Each exercise so far this week has been an invitation to listen. When do you listen to Christ and what form does your listening take? What affects whether you are all ears or hard of hearing?

Notice Peter's impulse to get busy, to say or do something, when given the gift of abiding for a time in God's transforming presence. What inside or outside you hinders you from remaining in God's presence for a time, listening to the voice of divine love?

Remain in the transfiguring Presence now for five to ten minutes. When other thoughts distract you, return your attention gently to God by refocusing on the presence of Christ.

EXERCISE 5   PRAYING WITH THE SPIRIT

*There is a prayer meeting constantly going on in our lives. . . . The Spirit intercedes deep within us, praying the prayer of Jesus, that we may be one and that this world will be mended.
(page 48)*

IF WE LISTEN BEYOND WHAT WE HAVE AND KNOW

Read Romans 8:21-27. The mending of the world can and must take many forms. Draw a small circle in your journal that represents the places in need of mending in your own life and relationships. Write a few words or draw some symbols in the circle that represent that brokenness. Around that circle draw a larger one that includes

WHAT CAN BE NOT JUST WHAT IS

your family and faith community. Put down words or symbols that represent the grief, hurt, or pain present among those close to you. Around that circle draw a third circle that represents the culture and society in which you live. In this circle include words or symbols that depict the bondage, decay, or pain within the larger society. Finally draw yet a larger circle that represents the earth and write or draw the hurts, destructions, wars, disease, and poverty that are in need of mending in the world.

As you look at the sorrow and hurt that is undeniably part of creation, join your prayers for hope and healing to the deep sighs of the Spirit. Pray for mending and reconciliation and the oneness of creation with the Creator.

Remember to review the insights recorded in your notebook or journal for the week in preparation for the group meeting.

Week 4

Experiencing the God Who Heals

Read James 5:13-20

A pastor was called to the hospital because an elderly woman in his congregation was seriously ill. When he arrived, he was surprised to find the woman sitting on the side of her bed, feet dangling over the edge. She was full of expectancy, but he wasn't.

He listened to her for several minutes, hoping then to get out of there without too much fuss and bother. But before he could leave, she asked him, "Will you pray for God to heal me?"

This was a daunting request, so in order to guard his reputation on one hand and to cover all the bases on the other, he offered a timid and tentative prayer. He prayed, "Lord, if it's your will, could you please bring your healing presence to bear upon this dear lady? And if it's not your will, Lord, will you just help us all to adjust to the situation?"

To his astonishment, the woman got up from her bed and began walking down the corridor shouting to everyone, "I'm well; I'm well! God has made me well!" The pastor was thunderstruck and wanted to get out of there as fast as he could. He rushed to the elevator and went down, got in his car, gripped the steering wheel, and prayed, "God, don't you ever do that to me again!"

Next time, not if only, is God's gracious answer to our admission of guilt, and nothing is more basic to the mending of the heart.

—John Claypool

We All Need Healing

Characterized by both adventure and mystery, healing is deeply relevant for us all. Every one of us hurt in some way or another. Some of us are caught up in broken relationships. Others struggle with addictions or compulsions of one kind or another. We all sit next to a pool of tears. Most profoundly, we all long to be holy and whole.

Every one of us needs God's healing presence in our lives. But we also need healing for our life together in the different communities from which we come. I come from a place with a deeply wounded history. South Africa has been torn apart by racism, discrimination, and prejudice. Because the scars are so deep, I cannot talk about healing in an individualistic way only. I have to talk about it in a way that brings healing to our common life together.

Healing touches us individually and touches our common life. With this in mind James writes to Christ-followers of his time. The early church was beginning to settle down, to have a regular ministry of healing. If someone was ill, they called for the elders who came and anointed them with oil. There were prayers and a time of confession to each other. Within that context of prayer, community, anointing of oil, confession, and forgiveness, there was an expectation that God's healing presence would be experienced.

When we bring these ingredients together into our worship, do we also have a lively expectation of God's healing presence? Often we look back and celebrate the wonderful things that God did in the past. Or we look forward and say God's going to do a wonderful thing in the future. But seldom do we expect God to step into our lives in the moment with healing presence and power. Our faith is like the White Queen's rule in *Through the Looking-glass:* "Jam to-morrow and jam yesterday—but never jam to-day."[1]

Becoming Vulnerable

Three lampposts from the scripture passage shed light on this mystery of healing. The first lamppost is this: *We open ourselves to God's*

> *It is my deepest conviction that if we will allow the risen Christ to transform our childish images of death into his vision of truth, he will also heal us from our grief in ways we do not expect.*
>
> —John Claypool

healing presence individually and in our life together when we allow ourselves to become vulnerable. Notice the clear instruction: "Are any among you sick? They should call for the elders of the church and have them pray over them" (v. 14). To ask is to become vulnerable, to experience our need, to admit our weakness.

When we read the scriptures, we are introduced to a God of power. God's power creates, redeems, liberates, and heals. I'm concerned, however, that we often speak about God's power in a triumphalistic way. We say that when God's power is at work, everything works out well. Testimonies to God's power often come across like that, especially when people giving those testimonies look good, are well-dressed, and have better teeth than us.

But what do these grandiose testimonies mean to parents whose child has leukemia? What do these testimonies to God's power mean to the thousands of young people in South Africa who are looking for a job? What do they mean to a mother of three, dying of breast cancer? What kind of God has been represented in these testimonies?

Although God is all powerful, that power is revealed in vulnerability, weakness, and suffering. That's the gospel secret. The God we worship has come to us in Jesus.

Look at the little baby lying in a manger in Bethlehem. He was born on the road, without even the basic comforts of an inn. Yet his birth attracted the veneration of both shepherds and kings. What a picture of both vulnerability and power.

Look at Jesus riding into Jerusalem on Palm Sunday. Did he ride on a white stallion with guns blazing and laser beams of supernatural energy emanating from him? No. Instead, he came on a donkey, unarmed, defenseless, weeping over the city. Yet people paved his path with palms and acclaimed him with hosannas. What a picture of both vulnerability and power.

Look at Jesus on the cross. Totally bound, weak, and broken, yet whispering God's forgiveness to those around him. What a picture of both vulnerability and power. The most transforming power we see in the Gospels is the power of crucified, vulnerable, suffering love. God's power is revealed in vulnerability.

The purpose of the dark night is purification or purgation, which leads to transformation and ultimately to freedom—freedom to be our true selves, to love and live in God, and to be filled with God.

—Jean M. Blomquist

It is God who invites us to participate in his mysterious will for the union of all things. God yearns for us to join in the divine love that longs for justice, and "works the redemption of the human race."

—Deborah Smith Douglas

Growing up, I was taught not to be vulnerable but to be strong, to call the shots, to be in control. My childhood hero was Superman. I longed to wear the red cape and the blue shirt with that big red *S*. The last thing in the world I wanted was to be vulnerable. And I wondered why I never experienced God's healing, life-giving, and -redeeming presence as an active reality in my life.

I remember the moment I began the journey into vulnerability. I was to speak to a group of business people in Port Elizabeth; and although I was feeling vulnerable, I didn't want anyone to know. I wanted to be in charge, in control. I was staying in the home of a colleague, and I got up very early that morning, anxiously feeling that everything depended on me. My friend George Irvine, an Irish minister, sensed that I was carrying too much. He took me outside just as the sun was coming up, put his arm around my shoulders, and said, "Trevor, look. The sun is coming up without you."

In that moment the Superman cape came off, and I began a descent into vulnerability and brokenness that continues to this day. I began to experience God's healing presence and power in new ways. I learned for myself how vulnerability opens our lives up to the possibilities of healing and new life.

September 11, 2001, was a moment of deep vulnerability for the United States as a nation. In that moment of deep vulnerability, the poorest of the poor in South Africa grieved with Americans and loved them. In suburbs, townships, cities, people came together, held services, and prayed for them. At that moment they didn't fear the United State's dominance. Their love came in response to a superpower's vulnerability.

We are all invited to become vulnerable, to take off our Superman and Superwoman capes, and to allow God to meet us in our deepest need. The simplest definition of the healing ministry of the Christian gospel is this: Jesus Christ meets us at the point of our deepest need.

Entering the Mystery

The second lamppost that we find in James 5 is this: *In order to open ourselves to God's healing presence and power, we need to be willing to enter into the mystery of prayer.* God heals in so many different ways. Sometimes God heals through doctors, nurses, and other health care professionals. God also heals through creation, through friendship, and through community. But I want to focus on the way God's healing power is released through prayer.

At this point I can go in one of two directions. I can give you techniques on healing prayer. I can explain how we say the right words and how to get the formula right. But I do not want to go this route. Rather, let me tell you the story of someone who began to pray. I'm speaking of the American social activist and evangelical preacher Tony Campolo. Wonderful things always seem to happen to him! Yet, he sees himself as only a beginner, just entering the mystery of healing prayer. He makes it a practice to anoint people with oil and pray for their healing, even though he says that nothing sensational happens. He prays because he believes God is the healer and because Jesus invites us to ask for healing.

A few years ago, Tony Campolo came to South Africa to speak. He tells this story about something that happened upon his return:

Coming into God's presence as sufferers, we can learn who we are, in our suffering and beyond suffering, and we can learn who God is, the God who suffers and the God who both transcends and transforms suffering.

—David Rensberger

> The next week I was back in the States and preaching at a church in Oregon. On impulse, as I ended the service I said to the congregation that if anyone wanted to remain behind for healing, I would be glad to pray with them. I told them they shouldn't expect much to happen, because nothing much happens when I pray, but if they wanted to give it a try, I'd be willing to pray as hard as I could. Surprisingly, about thirty people stayed behind and waited patiently as I prayed for one after the other.
>
> I did not want to do this healing thing fast, like some of the healers I see on television. I wanted to really talk to a person before I prayed and get a feel for what was on that person's heart. I wanted to hug each person and connect with him or her as deeply as I knew how. I did that with each of the people who stayed behind, and in each case I put some olive oil that I had brought along with me on each of their heads. It

took me more than an hour to pray through that little group. But I did it! What intrigued me was that most of the people who had come for healing had nothing physically wrong with them. One man needed healing for an addiction to pornography. One woman wanted healing for her marriage. Someone else asked healing for anger. But there were a few who did have physical illnesses.

Four days later I got a telephone call, and the woman at the other end said, "Tony, on Sunday you prayed for my husband. He had cancer."

When I heard the word "had" my heart quickened a bit. "Had cancer?" I asked.

The woman answered, "Well, he's dead now."

When she said that I thought to myself, *A lot of good I do.*

Then the woman said, "You don't understand. When my husband and I walked into that church on Sunday, he was angry with God. He had cancer and he knew he was going to be dead soon, and he hated God for letting it happen. He wanted to see his grandchildren grow up more than anything. At night he would lie in bed and curse God. It was horrible. And the angrier he got toward God, the meaner he was to everyone around him. It was unbearable to be in the same room with him. His nastiness just kept getting worse and worse and worse. But then you laid hands on him on Sunday morning and you prayed for him. When he walked out of church I knew there was something different. I could feel it. He was a different person. The last four days of our lives have been the best four days we've ever had together. We talked and laughed. We even sang hymns with each other. It was a good, good time."

She paused, then added something really profound. She said, "Tony, he wasn't cured, but he was healed." [2]

> We share in Christ's sufferings when we participate in his way of meeting suffering and its sources as we pursue, with him, the incarnation of the dream of the Kingdom.
>
> —Robert C. Morris

Tony mentions that when he prays for people, it sometimes seems as if nothing is happening; yet it is also obvious that something very deep is happening. He observes that people come to church hungering to be heard, to be touched, and to be healed. Tony's response is to ask if persons who come to hear him speak want to be prayed for, and then he prays for them.

Like Tony Campolo, let us also be drawn into the mystery of healing prayer. We don't need to worry about the right techniques or the right words or the right formulas. We simply enter into the experience of loving those around us, hearing their groans, weeping with those who weep, and praying with them.

Let us also pray like this for the healing of our communities. Walter Wink says magnificently and outrageously, "History belongs to the intercessors."[3] In South Africa we are free today as a country not only because of the liberation struggle but also because of the prayers that went up around the world in monasteries, convents, churches, and ordinary homes. Because of people who prayed year after year for the liberation of South Africa, we are free. The ministry of healing happened.

Confessing Our Sins

The final lamppost is this: *Healing is bound up with confession.* I have seen the power of this firsthand, in our life together as a nation and individually. In 1994 South Africa became a democracy. At that time our leaders faced the difficult question of what to do with all the atrocities that had been committed over the years. What were we going to do with those who had been involved in the violence, the killing, the murders?

Some people said we needed to hunt down those who did the damage, try them, and put them into prison. Others said we should let bygones be bygones, that since we're now a democracy, we should forget the past. But we couldn't do that. So God gave this country an idea. In 1994 we started the Truth and Reconciliation process. It lasted three years. This process offered victims an opportunity to tell their story in their own words. The commission proceedings were televised twenty-four hours a day so every South African could see the victims and hear them speak.

We heard the story of a young boy who said, "Can you find the remains of my father so we can have one bone to bring home and bury?" We heard the story of a sixteen-year-old girl who said, "Can you find who killed my dad in prison so I can learn to forgive him?"

On the other hand, those who had committed the atrocities and those who had benefited from years of privilege, and I am one of them, were able to confess what we did and how we benefited. Amnesty was given to all who testified in the process. I believe we saw

This unseen life is the Divine background—enormous, hidden, and near—a place where our spirits connect and are touched by the Eternal.

—Sue Monk Kidd

God at work in it. It was fallible, of course, and restitution remains to be made. But let our stories speak to your stories. Let God speak through our history to your history.

I've seen confession work for individuals also. Just the other day I told our congregation, "I'll be in the chapel from half-past five until half-past six on Wednesday evening. If you carry anything that you want to confess, it will be my privilege as a recovering sinner to be your priest."

I went there at half-past five and took a book with me to pass the hour. I never got to my book. It was a quarter until twelve before I went home. Streams of women and men stood in the line to confess secrets that they had carried for years. What a deep privilege it was to listen to people confess their sin, to offer these sins to God, and to share the word of forgiveness.

May we become a confessional people individually and in our life together. May we be surprised by the God of resurrection love who always brings us healing, even though we never know what it will look like in our lives or in the life of our nation.

In conclusion let me echo the words of Dr. Martin Luther King Jr.: God has a dream. It is a dream of a mended universe, a mended world, a mended people. God calls us into that dream to participate in it as partners. As Augustine, that great African saint, said, "Without God, we cannot. Without us, God will not."[4] God seeks to draw us into this dream of a healed creation, a healed universe, a healed world. Let us together bring healing in the name of Jesus Christ.

Were I a preacher, I should preach above all other things, the practice of the Presence of God: Were I a teacher, I should advise all the world to it; so necessary do I think it, and so easy.

—Brother Lawrence

DAILY EXERCISES

God hears our grief, pain, and anguish, offering a mysterious yet powerful healing presence in the midst of loss and sorrow. All people and the creation itself long for a healing touch, and followers of Christ are called to participate in that work. Such healing presence is not triumphal but vulnerable, not predictable but mysterious. Read Week 4, "Experiencing the God Who Heals," then work through the daily exercises for the week. Each day as you read and complete the exercises, place your sorrow, suffering, and need for healing into God's hands. Remember to reflect on your feelings, thoughts, and questions in your journal.

EXERCISE 1   EXAMINING YOUR SUFFERING

The simplest definition of the healing ministry of the Christian gospel is this: Jesus Christ meets us at the point of our deepest need. (page 58)

Read James 5:13-16. Today's exercise invites you to the spiritual practice of "examen" or as author Daniel Wolpert describes it, "examining our daily lives for signs of God's presence."[5] Two prerequisites exist for the practice of examen: (1) an intention to honor God's gracious revealing and (2) deep receptivity to what you discover. With these two postures in place you are ready to consider a time of suffering in your life and to see how God may have been present in the situation. Use all of your powers of observation, feeling, and imagination to experience this exercise.

Choose a time (a day, a week, a season) when your suffering and sorrow were significant. In your journal respond to the following questions:

- What happened in this time? How did you interpret the meaning of this period?

- What feelings emerge as you remember this time? What sustained you through the sorrow or suffering?

- Where do you perceive God at work in the situation?

- In retrospect, do you feel consolation or desolation about this period?

- What do you sense God is prompting you to learn from this time?

Pray for God's healing presence to give you consolation for your deepest needs.

EXERCISE 2   GOD'S HEALING PRESENCE

We open ourselves to God's healing presence individually and in our life together when we allow ourselves to become vulnerable. (pages 56–57)

Read James 5:13-16. Consider our society's attitudes toward vulnerability and strength as they surface in advertising, movies, video games, and political discourse. Make two columns in your journal. At the top of one write: "society's view of vulnerability and strength." At the top of the other column write: "gospel view of vulnerability and strength." In each column describe that viewpoint. You might also find a newspaper clipping or magazine cutout that illustrates your observations, place it in your journal, and bring it to this week's meeting.

Read the full passage again (verses 13–16) and list the various spiritual practices James commends. Which of the practices

- makes you most uncomfortable?

- calls for a new degree of risk and vulnerability?

- prompts you to try the practice as a means of grace and renewal?

Record your insights and experience in your journal.

EXERCISE 3   ENTERING THE MYSTERY OF PRAYER

In order to open ourselves to God's healing presence and power, we need to be willing to enter into the mystery of prayer. (page 59)

Read James 5:13-16. Then read once again Tony Campolo's story on pages 59–60. Write in your journal how the story affects you. For example, how do you feel about such bold and open-ended asking in prayer?

"Asking is the rule of the kingdom," C. H. Spurgeon once wrote.[6] Take a risk with God and ask for divine help where you see a need (personal or social) that concerns you deeply but for which you have never thought (or been willing) to go to God. Trust that God is already present to the situation, loves those concerned, and yearns for openings—such as your willingness to pray—through which to touch and transform.

Be sensitive to how the Lord of love bids you participate. Record your asking and the Lord's bidding.

EXERCISE 4   CONFESSING OUR SIN

Every one of us needs God's healing presence in our lives. But we also need healing for our life together. . . . Healing is bound up with confession. (pages 56, 61)

Read James 5:3-6. Trevor Hudson has said, "We let our institutions do our sinning for us." In what ways do we let ourselves off the hook when the institutions in our lives commit sins against the innocent and defenseless people of the world? What are the greatest challenges of institutional wrongdoing? How can committed individuals and groups nonetheless make a difference? Spend some time writing in your journal about these questions.

James called to confession those inside as well as outside the church, whose ways were working against God's will to mend the world. Where is confession needed today? How can it lead to a mending of the social order where the wounds are deepest? Reflect for a few moments on where you have a responsibility to urge such confession and reconciliation.

Sit quietly with Christ and listen. What would he add? Where would he comfort and where would he challenge?

EXERCISE 5   MENDING THE WORLD

God has a dream . . . of a mended universe, a mended world, a mended people. God calls us into that dream to participate in it as partners. (page 62)

Read James 5:7-11. In counseling the beloved to anticipate the "coming of the Lord [who] is near" (v. 8), James not only calls the church to "be patient" in waiting but to be participants in the healing work of God.

What is your dream of a healed and mended world? Describe or draw it in your journal.

Read the passage again. Note those actions James calls people to lay aside and those he calls people to take up as means of grace in Christ's healing work. Which of the practices described by the writer do you need to lay down? take up? Write them out.

To confirm your intent, choose a concrete action. For example,

- Find some small token or symbol of a practice you intend to let go or take up, to carry with you as a reminder.

- Tell someone you know of your intent.

- Identify someone you trust to whom you can confess your need.

Remember to review the insights recorded in your notebook or journal for the week in preparation for the group meeting.

Week 5

Discovering Community Together

Read 1 John 1:1-9

*I*t's been my privilege to be a pastor in many places in South Africa: in the rural areas of the Transkei, in the inner city of Johannesburg, and for the last twenty years in the sprawling townships and suburbs of the East Rand. I have discovered that one of the deep privileges of being a pastor is getting close to people—all kinds of people. People have become my living textbooks. From them I have learned many things. Perhaps one of the most crucial is that deep in the human heart there is a longing to belong, to connect, to be in communion, to be in the family.

The Western mind says, "I think, therefore I am." The African mind says, "I belong, therefore I am." Africans believe deeply that a person is only a person through other people. That is the way God has made us. God has made us to connect, to commune, to sit at the table together. It is not good for a human being to be alone, God says.

I have a hunch that if Jesus were to walk down the streets of your town or city today, he would look around at all those who are isolated and disconnected and say something like this: "Come to me all you who want to belong, and I will give you a table to sit around. Come to me all you who feel disconnected. Come to me all you who are lonely, cut off, rejected, and marginalized. Come to me. Come home. Come be part of the family that I want to share with you."

It is against that backdrop that we explore our scripture text from 1 John 1. As we stay close to the text, let's hear this invitation in a fresh, new way.

Justice wakes me from a walking sleep, the kind of self-centeredness that would leave me unaware of the humanity around me, until a poor woman taught me that being generous to the poor means being present to them and knowing them.

—Kristen Johnson Ingram

The Purpose of the Gospel

Notice something surprising about this text. John states the purpose of the gospel in one simple word—*fellowship*. In verse 3, John writes, "We declare to you what we have seen and heard so that you also may have fellowship with us." When I first read that, I was disappointed. Somehow the word *fellowship* has become weak. I think of fellowship as teas in church halls and shaking hands at church doors.

Did Jesus come and live, die, rise, ascend, and pour out his Spirit so that we could have teas in church halls and shake hands at church doors? I don't think so. We've got to reclaim the power of the word *fellowship*.

I know only one Greek word, *koinonia*. It's a rich and a rigorous word. It's also not a religious word. It comes from the common language of the people and simply means "a sharing life"—a sharing of our personal lives, our relational lives, our economic lives, our common lives.

When Jesus spoke from the cross to Mary and John, he said to Mary, "Here is your son." To John he said, "Here is your mother" (John 19:26-27). When John took Mary from the foot of the cross, he didn't take her to a prayer meeting but into his home. He shared his life with her.

That's why Jesus came and lived, rose, ascended, and poured out his Spirit—so that he could call us out of our individualism into a rich common life. It's lovely having Communion together, but in many churches it's you with your little tumbler and me with my little tumbler. What a shame that we who share in the common cup should be so separated. Jesus calls us to leave our own little tumblers and share in a common meal and a common cup.

Let me ask: Is this purpose of the gospel being fulfilled in your congregation? It's not so much that a church looks for its mission. Instead, God is looking for a church that will fulfill *God's* mission. Will yours be that kind of congregation in which this common life can be made known and demonstrated?

It is a sin to live without fighting with all our might, where we are, for more justice in the world.
—Michel Quoist

Horizontal and Vertical

Notice the different dimensions of this common life. There is a horizontal relationship: "We declare to you what we have seen and heard so that you also may have fellowship with us" (v. 3). And in that verse there is also a vertical relationship: "Our fellowship is with the Father and with his Son Jesus Christ." Fellowship is cross-shaped; we need both the vertical and the horizontal. Otherwise we lose the cross.

As we have said earlier, when we open our lives to Jesus, he never comes alone. He brings his friends, who have become a new kind of family, with him. Let that image instruct our journey as congregations. We always journey with Jesus in the presence of other human beings. And so often these people with whom we travel are different from us.

My wife, Debbie, and I had four weeks leave from our congregation last year. We decided to use that time to worship in other churches. On the first Sunday we visited the Anglicans. There we experienced smells and bells, robes and liturgies; everything went decently and in order. As the priest put the wafer on my tongue and held the cup, Christ was present.

The next Sunday Debbie and I visited the Pentecostals. We stood for forty-five minutes, singing one song after another. Then the preacher "let it rip" for another forty-five minutes. And Christ was present.

The third week I visited the Quakers. In my heart I'm a closet Quaker. You know what they do—nothing. For one hour I sat with people from all over Africa, from Mozambique, Angola, and the Congo. We sat in the silence and were only allowed to speak if we could improve on the silence, so no one spoke. And Christ was present.

On the fourth Sunday we went to a Methodist church. You know what it's like with the Methodists—a Dagwood sandwich: hymn, prayer, hymn, prayer, hymn, prayer, hymn, sermon, prayer. And Christ was present there, too!

In those four weeks I gained a sense of the treasures of the streams of the Christian family. We live in our own little ghettos, so impoverished because of our small hearts and because we don't want to

The Christ-centered community . . . is alive and open to the Spirit, and the openness and loving acceptance of one another that is essential to our life together. Truth and love are not antithetical, but to incorporate them in our care for each other can be hard work.

—Margaret Guenther

open them to the family. The streams are rich and deep: contemplative, social justice, evangelical, sacramental, word-centered.[1] They are all there, rich and colorful, waiting for us to open our hearts to it all.

Walking in God's Light

This kind of shared life invites us to walk in the light. If we don't walk in the light, as John puts it, we don't share in a common life. John invites us out of our darkness to walk in the light in one another's presence. That doesn't mean we have to be perfect. It doesn't mean we have it all together. It means we are willing to be vulnerable, open, and honest with others.

In my church on a Thursday night, we have an Alcoholics Anonymous meeting. A lot of my friends are there, so I often put my head in to say hi. Everyone is smoking, and I envision smoke going into the curtains and ash falling on the carpets. Then a man stands up and says, "My name is Billy, and I'm an alcoholic, and this week has been a terrible week for me. I've been terrible to live with. I've spoken badly to my kids and to my wife." And then Tessa stands up and says, "My name is Tessa, and I'm an alcoholic, and I've been back on the booze this week, and I'm really in trouble." And then Susan stands up and says, "My name is Susan, and I lost it this week. I absolutely lost it. I said things that I've never said before." I think to myself as I hear this, *what a mess in my church hall.*

Then I go next door to the fellowship hall. There I find a group of church members sitting in a circle "doing church," speaking in niceties but avoiding telling the truth. It looks very holy. I sometimes suspect I see a glow around those who are seated there. Although it looks holy, it somehow also seems dishonest.

I go out to the parking lot, and I ask, "Jesus, where do you hang out in this church? Do you hang out in the AA hall or the fellowship hall?" I've never heard an audible answer, but I have a hunch that Jesus would say to me, "I hang out in the AA hall because people there are speaking truth and seeking help, and that is where God is at work purifying people from their sins."

> *Living together as the body of Christ requires intentional, compassionate care for one another. We need the support of companions on this journey, and when we are willing to serve rather than to look for self-satisfaction, the community grows more robust.*
>
> —Elizabeth J. Canham

It's when we walk in the light of simple honesty that the redemptive power of God in Christ is released. When we take off the halos, when we allow ourselves to be known as broken human beings, as recovering sinners, in that moment of walking in the light, we experience the redemptive power of Jesus.

Fellowship as a Gift of the Spirit

In 2 Corinthians 13:13, Paul gives a triune blessing: "May the grace of our Lord Jesus Christ, the love of God, and the fellowship of the Holy Spirit be with you all" (NLT). I can almost imagine him saying, "I want to get to essentials now, no more nonessentials. What is the most important thing that I can say about Jesus? Grace. What is the most important thing I can say about the Father? Love."

What's the most important thing I can say about the Holy Spirit? Power? Tongues? Gifts? No. Fellowship! Yes, fellowship is the deepest work of God's Spirit. The Spirit of God is drawing us all of the time into a common life with one another. That is the central work of God's Spirit—creating community.

Are we going to resist or respond to the Spirit? Are we going to quench the Spirit or allow the Spirit to draw us and our congregations into a new level of shared living? Are we going to allow the purpose of the gospel to be fulfilled in our lives? Let's respond positively and wholeheartedly to what the Spirit may be inviting us to do.

Our responses may look different. For some it may mean saying, "I'm going to put my own weight down in one local faith community. Church hopping is over. I am going to own this messy community as my community." For others it may mean becoming part of a small group such as *Companions in Christ,* and saying, "Let's journey together. Let's go beyond the superficial. Let's go into the depths." For some it will mean getting honest, becoming vulnerable. If we don't get used to walking in the light, then heaven is going to be hell for us. In heaven the lights are always on.

For some it will mean extending an invitation to Christian community in a new way, saying, "The table is ready. Come." A little church

It is a peace not constructed by tough competition, hard thinking, and individual stardom, but rooted in simply being present to each other, a peace that speaks about the first love of God by which we are all held and a peace that keeps calling us to community, a fellowship of the weak.

—Henri J. M. Nouwen

on the edge of Johannesburg was dwindling in membership. Last year on the Thursday and Friday before Easter, they went out into the streets with an invitation to the blind, crippled, lame, and outsider. It said simply, "You are invited to a banquet in the name of Jesus Christ at the Berea Methodist Church. Come as you are." On Easter Sunday this little church, which was dying, was filled around the table. Professors sat down with prostitutes. Blacks sat with whites. Gays sat with straights. God's people were together. One young person who was there said, "Today I know that Jesus is risen."

God's purpose for humanity is the creation of inclusive community where all are welcomed and where the central inhabitant is the glorious figure of Jesus Christ. God is looking for a people who will reign with God forever. Wal-Mart will pass away. Citibank will pass away. The IRS will pass away. The American dream will pass away. But God's people will live forever. Will you become part of that people whom God is creating?

DAILY EXERCISES

In a world where rugged individualism is highly valued, discovering and participating in a genuine community of Christian fellowship may be among the most radical acts of our age. One of the primary ends of the gospel is to befriend and include all who are willing to become Christ-followers around the communal table. As you read this week's article and exercises, keep in mind those who are your companions in fellowship and ministry. Express your thanks to God for calling you into a place of belonging, and seek ways to extend that invitation to those who live on the margins in isolation, rejection, or despair. Read Week 5, "Discovering Community Together" before working through the daily exercises. Keep your journal or notebook close at hand so you can write down feelings, thoughts, impressions, and questions that arise while you read the article and complete the exercises. Remain open to the Spirit's prompting as your week unfolds.

EXERCISE 1   THE JOY OF BELONGING

John states the purpose of the gospel in one simple word—fellowship.... That's why Jesus came and lived, rose, ascended, and poured out his Spirit—so that he could call us out of our individualism into a rich common life. (page 68)

Read 1 John 1:1-4. There are many kinds of fellowship in this world, each based on a different point of commonality, for better or worse. The writer of First John is declaring the power of shared experience in a genuine, close fellowship with Jesus Christ and God the Creator. The experience is one of a joy that wants to be shared.

Think back through any experiences you may have had of genuine community and Christian fellowship. What particular characteristics of fellowship do you recall as most significant? What most impressed you? What arises from fellowship with God in Christ that is transforming, that Jesus would live and die for? Record your memories and observations in your journal.

Close your time of remembrance with a prayer of thanksgiving for any joys of community that you have experienced.

EXERCISE 2   FULFILLING THE GOSPEL

Is this purpose of the gospel being fulfilled in your congregation?
(page 68)

Read 1 John 1:1-9. Based on John's witness in this New Testament letter, the purpose of the gospel is fulfilled when the church becomes a cross-shaped fellowship, a fellowship of Christians that is opening up to God (vertical) and out to people (horizontal) in the love of Christ.

Draw a diagram of a cross as a way of imaging the cross-shaped fellowship Christ creates. Near the center name the groups or ministries in your church in which you see the cross-shaped quality of Christian fellowship being fulfilled.

Along the vertical and horizontal lines write the names of groups or experiences in your church that express either the vertical or horizontal dimensions of Christ's life but maybe don't accomplish both.

Now ponder your picture alongside this question: "Is this purpose of the gospel being fulfilled in your congregation?" What are your thoughts? What is a possible next step to becoming a church truly fulfilling God's mission of creating a new kind of world, beginning with the fellowship of your faith community? What might God be calling your church to do? Jot down your thoughts in your journal.

EXERCISE 3   HANGING OUT WITH JESUS

"Jesus, where do you hang out in this church?" (page 70)

Read 1 John 1:1-9. John writes, "Truly our fellowship is with the Father and with his Son Jesus Christ." As the disciples learned, fellowship with Jesus involved fellowship with all kinds of people.

Seek to enter more deeply into fellowship with God, by opening yourself to the guidance of the Holy Spirit. Suppose that the Holy Spirit asks you to start by spending time in fellowship with the Son Jesus Christ. Prayerfully imagine what it would mean to tag along with Jesus as he enters your situation. Where would Jesus go; who would Jesus fellowship with; and what would he do? Now ask: "Jesus, where do you hang out in this church?" Pay attention to what comes to mind. What qualities of fellowship stand out for you in those places? Record your thoughts.

Decide today to act on one thing Jesus might do if he were in your situation, as an expression of your desire to be in fellowship with him.

EXERCISE 4   WALKING IN THE LIGHT

This kind of shared life invites us to walk in the light. . . . It means we are willing to be vulnerable, open, and honest with others. (page 70)

Read 1 John 1:5-7. For John the practice of "walking in the light" is the key to true community as God intends it. To help you pray about walking in the light, use the method of *lectio divina* to engage this passage.

As you read aloud the passage the first time, allow your mind to be drawn to a word, image, or phrase. Hold onto that word in a few moments of silence following your first reading, and record it in your journal.

As you read the passage again, reflect on the meaning of the word, phrase, or image that you caught onto the first time. Meditate on the possibilities and see where it leads you. What horizon does it open up for your own journey of faith?

As you read the passage a final time, respond to God in conversation about the direction you find yourself going, and answer these questions: How is God's Spirit speaking to me? How has my understanding about "walking in the light" been nurtured or challenged? To what am I being called? Note your responses in your journal.

Commit this day to the practice of walking in the light.

EXERCISE 5   EXPERIENCING *KOINONIA*

The Spirit of God is drawing us all of the time into a common life with one another. That is the central work of God's Spirit— creating community. Are we going to resist or respond to the Spirit? (page 71)

Read 1 John 1:1-9. John's letter models several spiritual practices by which the Holy Spirit creates genuine community among us: faith sharing (v. 1), letter writing (v. 4), listening to God (v. 5), walking in the light (v. 7), truth telling (v. 8), and confession (9). What additional practices in your experience foster community in Christ?

What spiritual practices do you most need as you try to live in *koinonia* with your faith community? What practices are most needed in your church at this time as means of grace, through which the Holy Spirit can create or restore genuine community in Christ?

Spend a few moments in prayer for your faith community or group, opening to the guidance of the Holy Spirit. Where is the Spirit leading the community? Where is the hidden resistance in you or among you? What action is the Spirit prompting you to take as a member of the community?

Note your thoughts in your journal.

Remember to review the insights recorded in your notebook or journal for the week in preparation for the group meeting.

Pre-Retreat Daily Exercises

*T*he last six weeks have been an invitation to renewal and recommitment as a Christ-follower. In this brief journey we have considered who we are as beloved children of God and how we might become genuine followers of Christ, who is ever willing to be our mentor. We have pondered who the friends of Jesus are and where he might hang out in our churches and the world today. We have considered the deep pain and hope in our lives and the lives of others and explored how God stands willing to offer healing presence through the community of faithful Christ-followers. This week we bring our work to a close with a Pilgrimage and Retreat of Pain and Hope. As you may recall from reading the article "Listening to the Groans," Trevor Hudson made annual Pilgrimages of Pain and Hope into the townships of South Africa with his own faith community. They went not as tourists but as pilgrims to be present with people, to hear their stories, to be open to God's presence and prompting. The Closing Pilgrimage and Retreat is designed to offer an abbreviated version of just such an experience. The pilgrimage and retreat deserve careful preparation and meaningful reflection. Already the group has been working and planning the various components of the closing event. This week the focus will be not only on finalizing details of preparation, but also on individual spiritual preparation.

The following daily exercises offer guidance as you prepare your heart and mind to make a Pilgrimage of Pain and Hope. It will help you to think about your approach to the visit, your ability to listen and be present, your powers of attentiveness for noticing what you see and hear, and your deep hopes for change. Keep your journal or notebook nearby so you can record thoughts, ideas, feelings, and questions that come to mind as you complete these exercises.

EXERCISE 1   FINDING THE PILGRIM POSTURE

Read John 14:4-6. Jesus told the disciples that he was and is the Way to the fullness of life. The way of Jesus was one of entering into the suffering and anguish of humanity in the love of God. In order to see, hear, and understand both the pain and hope of our sisters and brothers, we are invited to make a pilgrimage. To see not only the underside of the human condition but also the amazing transcendence, we must approach our task not as missionaries or tourists but as pilgrims of the Way. In your journal write two headings: "tourist" and "pilgrim." Under each word list the things that come to mind. Compare and contrast the two lists.

Pilgrims are receptive to the experiences of their journey and even willing to be transformed by what they encounter. According to Trevor Hudson, "Their posture before the mystery of life is one of vulnerable openness, nonpossessive engagement, reverent participation, and childlike wonder."[1] What attitudes, feelings, or past experiences might block you from approaching life this way? What might keep you from "vulnerable openness" to the pilgrimage planned for this week? Record your thoughts in your journal. Pray for God's help in finding and holding the posture of a pilgrim.

EXERCISE 2   LEARNING TO BE PRESENT

Read Psalm 139:1-6. God is present to us in profound and mysterious ways. The psalmist admits the ways of God are too high to attain. How could we ever be as present to one another as God is to us?

Being present to one another as God is present to us starts with showing up and making the effort. It also means not being preoccupied by distractions and worries of past or future. Sometimes our minds have to catch up with our bodies, our mental presence with our physical presence. To help with being fully present, try the following exercise. Sit for five minutes and simply be present to your circumstances and surroundings.[2] Look, listen, and take in all that is around you. Be present to the room or visible space where you are. Notice the small details. After five minutes record what you notice.

Trevor Hudson says, "Being present involves letting go of our constant preoccupations, immersing ourselves in the here and now, and giving ourselves wholeheartedly to whatever is at hand."[3] This kind of presence takes patience and disciplined practice. Each day of the remaining week you will be invited to continue practicing your ability to be present in the moment.

Spend the last five minutes of this daily exercise being present to God by addressing God in your journal.

EXERCISE 3   CULTIVATING DEEP LISTENING

Read Psalm 46. As you read, notice the noisy context of verse 10, "Be still and know that I am God,": desolation, wars, bows and shields. Now turn your attention once again to your immediate surroundings. Involve your ears as well as your eyes. Note the sounds you hear and record them in your journal. Listen for sounds hidden under other sounds (humming equipment, chirping birds, or buzzing bugs). Even in the midst of war and confusion the Lord's message is "Be still and know that I am God." We are called to listen both to our fellow human beings and to the stillness of God.

In his book *A Mile in My Shoes* Trevor Hudson identifies three simple guidelines for becoming a better listener: (1) stop talking, (2) give attention to the speaker, and (3) communicate an understanding of what is shared.[4] Which of these guidelines is the easiest for you? Which poses the greatest challenge? What distracts you most from listening deeply? Ponder these questions in your journal and ask God's help in making you a better listener.

As you go through your day practice this quality of listening. Focus on listening more deeply to people whose paths you cross. What happens when you stop talking, give your full attention, and reflect what you have heard?

EXERCISE 4   PREPARING TO NOTICE

Read 1 John 1:1-4. As you read, notice the way John and other witnesses experience God's reality in what they had heard, seen, and touched.

Again spend five minutes in the discipline of being present to your concrete surroundings. What do you notice?

We are often better at noticing things in hindsight than in the moment. This seems especially true of our ability to notice the presence and prompting of God. One way to improve our powers of noticing *in the moment* is to practice looking back and taking note.

Spend a few moments looking back over the journey of the last six weeks. Write in your journal answers to these questions:
- What moments stand out for you and why?
- What has changed in your way of thinking or feeling related to your life as a Christ-follower?
- Where in the process of reading, reflecting, sharing, and worshiping has the presence of God been most palpable for you?
- What would be your greatest joy to share with others? Pause to give thanks to God for the gifts you have received.

EXERCISE 5   HOPING FOR TRANSFORMATION

Begin your time with the exercise of spending five minutes attending to your surroundings. How have your skills of being present changed or improved over the last few days?

Read Mark 1:14-15. Jesus often called those he met to follow and to repent, which can be understood as a call to turn around and change your whole way of thinking. This call to radical change, however, is no guarantee that transformation will happen. We can plan for pilgrimage. We can plan for encounter and reflection, but we cannot assure transformation. Trevor Hudson observes, "Transformation into greater Christlikeness comes as a gift to those who generously open to the Holy Spirit."[5] This is a gift we can seek and hope for by opening ourselves to the grace of the Spirit.

In preparation for the pilgrimage, write in your journal your thoughts on these three questions:

- What is your hope for the situation and the people to which your group will be making a pilgrimage? Name your hopes in the form of a poem, prayer, or simply free-form thoughts.
- What fears do you bring with you to this experience?
- What is your prayer that expresses both the hopes and the fears to God?

Remember to review the insights recorded in your notebook or journal for the week in preparation for the Closing Pilgrimage and Retreat.

THE WAY OF TRANSFORMING DISCIPLESHIP
CLOSING PILGRIMAGE AND RETREAT SCHEDULE OUTLINE

FRIDAY EVENING

6:00	Gather for dinner (potluck or other simple fare)
7:00	Opening worship
7:15	Sharing insights from the week
8:00	Overview of the pilgrimage site and plans for Saturday
8:15	Deeper Exploration
9:00	Evening prayers
9:15	Dismiss

SATURDAY MORNING

8:00	Morning prayers (coffee, tea, or juice may be made available)
8:30	Travel to the pilgrimage site
9:00	Meet with residents and caregivers at the site
12:00	Shared lunch at the pilgrimage site
1:00	Return travel to the retreat site
1:30	Individual reflection and journaling time
2:15	Group reflection
3:10	Letter writing
3:45	Closing worship and communion or Love Feast
4:15	Dismiss

Annotated Resource List

*T*he following list contains information about the *Companions in Christ* series, books that may be excerpted from in *The Way of Transforming Discipleship,* and resources that expand on the material in this book. As you read and share with your group, you may find some material that particularly challenges or helps you. If you wish to pursue individual reading on your own or if your small group wishes to follow up with additional resources, this list may be useful. Unless otherwise indicated, these books can be ordered at www.upper-room.org/bookstore/ or by calling 1-800-972-0433.

THE COMPANIONS IN CHRIST SERIES

Companions in Christ: A Small-Group Experience in Spiritual Formation (Participant's Book)
by Gerrit Scott Dawson, Adele J. Gonzalez, E. Glenn Hinson, Rueben P. Job, Marjorie J. Thompson, and Wendy M. Wright
0-8358-0914-5

Companions in Christ: A Small-Group Experience in Spiritual Formation (Leader's Guide)
by Stephen D. Bryant, Janice T. Grana, and Marjorie J. Thompson
0-8358-0915-3

The Way of Grace (Participant's Book)
by John Indermark
0-8358-9878-4

The Way of Grace (Leader's Guide)
by Marjorie J. Thompson and Melissa Tidwell
0-8358-9879-2

√ *The Way of Blessedness* (Participant's Book)
by Marjorie J. Thompson and Stephen D. Bryant
0-8358-0992-7
The Way of Blessedness (Leader's Guide)
by Stephen D. Bryant
0-8358-0994-3

√ *The Way of Forgiveness* (Participant's Book)
by Marjorie J. Thompson
0-8358-0980-3
The Way of Forgiveness (Leader's Guide)
by Stephen D. Bryant and Marjorie J. Thompson
0-8358-0981-1

Exploring the Way: An Introduction to the Spiritual Journey (Participant's Book) by Marjorie J. Thompson
0-8358-9806-7
Exploring the Way: An Introduction to the Spiritual Journey (Leader's Guide)
by Marjorie J. Thompson and Stephen D. Bryant
0-8358-9807-5

The Way of the Child (Available June 2006)
by Wynn McGregor

Leader's Guide and Sessions	$25	0-8358-9824-5
Family Booklet	$5	0-8358-9839-3
Resource Booklet	$6	0-8358-9825-3
Music CD	$15	0-8358-9845-8
Training DVD	$15	0-8358-9846-6
Church Pack	$150	0-8358-9847-4

The Way of the Child focuses on the spiritual formation of children ages 6–11. Part of the *Companions in Christ* series, it helps children learn and experience spiritual practices that will lead them into a deeper awareness of God's presence in their lives. The Leader's Guide includes five chapters on the spiritual nature of children and theory of faith formation as well as thirty-nine sessions to use with groups of children. There are enough sessions to use from September through May in Sunday school or weekday or weeknight settings. It is also designed for short-term use such as during Advent, Lent, or other special times of the year.

Journal: A Companion for Your Quiet Time
Introduction by Anne Broyles
Provides generous space for writing, faint lines to guide your journaling, and a layflat binding. Many pages contain inspirational thoughts to encourage your time of reflection.
0-8358-0938-2

The Faith We Sing
A feast of contemporary songs in a range of styles, this hymnal supplement is available in a variety of print editions and has a CD Accompaniment Edition as well. To see the full range of *The Faith We Sing* products or to place an order visit www.cokesbury.com or call 1-800-672-1789.

KNOWING WHO WE ARE

Wrestling with Grace: A Spirituality for the Rough Edges of Daily Life
by Robert Corin Morris
A how-to manual about loving God, yourself, others, and the world around you.
0-8358-0985-4

The Workbook on Lessons from the Saints by Maxie Dunnam
An eight-week study that makes the connection between our lives and the lives of great spiritual writers of the past, including Martin Luther, Francis of Assisi, and Thérèse of Lisieux.
0-8358-0965-X

Yearning for God: Reflections of Faithful Lives
by Margaret Ann Crain and Jack Seymour
Yearning for God explores the stories of more than forty faithful individuals, offering an excellent group discussion guide with thought-provoking questions. A significant resource for all those who search for meaning through God's presence in a troubled world.
0-8358-0991-9

Remembering Your Story: Creating Your Own Spiritual Autobiography (revised edition)
by Richard L. Morgan
A guide for discovering the story of our spiritual journey and sharing that story with others. Leader's Guide (0-8358-0964-1) available.
0-8358-0963-3

CHANGING FROM THE INSIDE

Turn Toward Promise: The Prophets and Spiritual Renewal by John Indermark
Indermark draws on the stories of Isaiah, Jeremiah, and Ezekiel to take readers on a journey of spiritual renewal that is relevant today.
0-8358-9887-3

Living Your Heart's Desire: God's Call and Your Vocation
by Gregory S. Clapper
Discover a variety of visions of what it means to lead a life of Christian faithfulness—regardless of how you earn a paycheck.
0-8358-9805-9

Creating a Life with God: The Call of Ancient Prayer Practices
by Daniel Wolpert
This book offers the opportunity to learn and adopt twelve prayer practices, including solitude and silence, *lectio divina*, the Jesus prayer, creativity, journaling, and more.
0-8358-9855-5

Jesus, Our Spiritual Director: A Pilgrimage Through the Gospels
by Wendy Miller
Miller demonstrates the deep biblical roots of spiritual direction in the ministry of Jesus, his disciples, and Christians today.
0-8358-9876-8

LISTENING TO THE GROANS

Listening at Golgotha: Jesus' Words from the Cross by Peter Storey
The last utterances of Christ from the cross cast light on his saving work and invite us to engage in the depths of his suffering. These meditations were born from Storey's ministry under apartheid in South Africa.
0-8358-9884-9

Ashes Transformed: Healing from Trauma: 43 Stories of Faith
by Tilda Norberg
Forty-three poignant stories told by people who experienced God's presence in connection with the terrorist attacks on the U.S. on Sept. 11, 2001.
0-8358-0986-2

Heart Whispers: Benedictine Wisdom for Today by Elizabeth J. Canham
Insights from Benedictine spirituality to help us realize the need for faithful living and balance in today's stressful world. Leader's Guide (0-8358-0893-9) with ten sessions available.
0-8358-0892-0

A Turbulent Peace: The Psalms for Our Time by Ray Waddle
Waddle writes about each of the 150 Psalms and helps us discover the comfort and the inspiration found there, particularly in light of the anxieties and stresses of living today.
0-8358-9873-3

EXPERIENCING THE GOD WHO HEALS

An Adventure in Healing and Wholeness: The Healing Ministry of Christ in the Church Today by James K. Wagner
A seven-session study of the holistic approach to health and of the relationship between prayer and healing. Also in Spanish and Korean.
0-8358-0689-8

Stretch Out Your Hand: Exploring Healing Prayer by Tilda Norberg and Robert D. Webber
In this exploration of God's healing love for individuals, institutions, and communities, we find an honest examination of the many difficult questions about prayer and the role of faith in healing.
0-8358-0872-6

The Spiritual Heart of Your Health: A Devotional Guide on the Healing Stories of Jesus by James K. Wagner
Wagner looks at thirty healing stories of Jesus from the Gospels. More than offering a Bible study, Wagner teaches a process to pray for healing as we read and study these passages. Styled as a workbook for either individual or small-group study.
0-8358-0958-7

Prayer, Stress, and Our Inner Wounds by Flora Slosson Wuellner
Prayers and spiritual exercises to help us receive God's love—and heal physical pain, painful memories, and the pain of uncertainty and stress.
0-8358-0501-8

DISCOVERING COMMUNITY TOGETHER

Yours Are the Hands of Christ: The Practice of Faith by James C. Howell
A fresh look at familiar moments in the life of Jesus, this book also draws on the lives of saints through history who are great examples to us of being the hands of Christ today.
0-8358-0867-X

The Soul of Tomorrow's Church: Weaving Spiritual Practices in Ministry Together by Kent Ira Groff
Brims with insights about crisis and ministry and offers practical solutions. The challenge for tomorrow's church is not to focus on new structures or programs but to focus on ways to infuse ministry with new life.
0-8358-0927-7

Cultivating Christian Community by Thomas R. Hawkins
Hawkins believes that healthy Christian community is marked by six qualities: practices hospitality, is centered on Christ, practices the means of grace, occurs when we find healing and wholeness, invites us to discover our unique gifts, and equips us to live out our baptismal covenant.
0-88177-327-1

Discovering Community: A Meditation on Community in Christ
by Stephen V. Doughty
Doughty looks at what it means to be a part of the community of Christ through a number of lenses, focusing on the diverse ways and places in which Christian disciples grow.
0-8358-0870-X

CLOSING PILGRIMAGE AND RETREAT

A Mile in My Shoes: Cultivating Compassion by Trevor Hudson
Experience the three essential ingredients of pilgrimage: encounter, reflection, and transformation. Leads individuals and groups as they consider becoming pilgrims in daily life.
0-8358-9815-6

Spiritual Life in the Congregation: A Guide for Retreats by Rueben P. Job
Offers an easy-to-use, step-by-step approach to successful spiritual formation retreats for almost every group in the congregation, including churchwide, youth, older adults, personal, private, and "action" retreats.
0-8358-0818-1

OTHER RESOURCES OF INTEREST

The Upper Room Dictionary of Christian Spiritual Formation
by Keith Beasley-Topliffe
Nearly five hundred articles cover the people, methods, and concepts associated with spiritual formation with a primary emphasis on prayer and other spiritual disciplines.
0-8358-0993-5

Alive Now
With a mix of prayers, award-winning poetry, stories of personal experience, and contributions from well-known authors, *Alive Now* offers readers a fresh perspective on living faithfully. Available as an individual subscription or group order.

Weavings: A Journal of the Christian Spiritual Life
Through thoughtful exploration of enduring spiritual life themes, *Weavings* offers trustworthy guidance on the journey to greater love for God and neighbor.

Notes

Week 1: Knowing Who We Are

1. "Just as I Am, Without One Plea," lyrics by Charlotte Elliott, *The United Methodist Hymnal* (Nashville, Tenn.: United Methodist Publishing House, 1989), no. 357.

2. Henri Nouwen, *Life of the Beloved: Spiritual Living in a Secular World* (New York: Crossroad Publishing Co., 2001), 57–59.

Week 2: Changing from the Inside

1. Anthony C. LoBaido, "Child-rape Epidemic in South Africa," WorldNet-Daily.com (Dec. 26, 2001).

2. E. Stanley Jones, *Mahatma Gandhi: An Interpretation* (New York: Abingdon-Cokesbury Press, 1948), 54.

3. Richard Rohr, *Everything Belongs: The Gift of Contemplative Prayer* (New York: Crossroad Publishing Co., 1999), 140.

4. "Just as I Am, Without One Plea," *The United Methodist Hymnal*, no. 357.

5. Anthony de Mello, *Taking Flight: A Book of Story Meditations* (New York: Image Books, 1988), 114.

6. See "Defining Moments: Desmond Tutu," *BBC News World Edition*, July 9, 2003, http://newswww.bbc.net.uk.

Week 3: Listening to the Groans

1. Opponents of Nazi interference in German churches, including Bonhoeffer, established a new Confessing Church in 1934. The reality never matched the vision, however, and eventually the church became immobilized as Hitler gained power.

2. Dietrich Bonhoeffer, *Life Together* (New York: Harper & Brothers, 1954), 97–98.

3. "I Have Decided to Follow Jesus," *The Baptist Hymnal* (Nashville, Tenn.: Convention Press, 1991), no. 305.

4. "Turn Your Eyes upon Jesus," lyrics by Helen H. Lemmel, *The United Methodist Hymnal* (Nashville, Tenn.: United Methodist Publishing House, 1989), no. 349.

5. See Margaret Cropper, *Life of Evelyn Underhill* (New York: Harper, 1958), 69.

6. "From a Distance," lyrics by Julie Gold, *Bette Midler: Greatest Hits—Experience the Divine* (Atlantic/Wea, 1993).

7. Dietrich Bonhoeffer, "Christians and Pagans," *Letters and Papers from Prison*, ed. Eberhard Bethge (New York: Macmillan, 1972), 349.

WEEK 4: EXPERIENCING THE GOD WHO HEALS

1. Lewis Carroll, *Through the Looking-glass and What Alice Found There* (New York: William Morrow and Company, 1993), 94.

2. Tony Campolo, *Let Me Tell You a Story* (Nashville: Word Publishing, 2000), 34–36.

3. Walter Wink, *The Powers That Be: Theology for a New Millennium* (New York: Random House, 1999), 187.

4. Augustine, quoted in "Bishop Graham Walden," a lecture given by David Chislett SSC at Aldinga in the Diocese of The Murray on May 18, 2001. http://www.all-saintsbrisbane.com/03_news/bishopwalden. htm

5. Daniel Wolpert, *Creating a Life with God: The Call of Ancient Prayer Practices* (Nashville, Tenn.: Upper Room Books, 2003), 76.

6. C. H. Spurgeon, quoted in Richard J. Foster, *Prayer: Finding the Heart's True Home* (San Francisco: HarperSanFrancisco, 1992), 179.

WEEK 5: DISCOVERING COMMUNITY TOGETHER

1. See Richard J. Foster, *Streams of Living Water: Celebrating the Great Traditions of Christian Faith* (San Francisco: HarperSanFrancisco, 2001).

PRE-RETREAT DAILY EXERCISES

1. Trevor Hudson, *A Mile in My Shoes* (Nashville, Tenn.: Upper Room Books, 2005), 31.

2. Hudson, *A Mile in My Shoes*, 31–32.

3. Ibid, 30.

4. Ibid 33–35.

5. Ibid, 21–22.

Sources and Authors
of Marginal Quotations

PREPARATORY MEETING

Luther E. Smith Jr., "Home on the Road," *Weavings* (Nov/Dec 2001): 13.

Michael Downey, "Gift's Constant Coming," *Weavings* (Nov/Dec 1999): 32.

Evelyn Underhill, *The Soul's Delight: Selected Writings of Evelyn Underhill*, ed. Keith Beasley-Topliffe (Nashville, Tenn.: Upper Room Books, 1998), 57.

WEEK 1: KNOWING WHO WE ARE

Joan D. Chittister, *Scarred by Struggle, Transformed by Hope* (Grand Rapids, Mich.: William B. Eerdmans Publishing Company, 2003), 24.

Hildegard of Bingen, *The Wisdom of Hildegard of Bingen*, comp. Fiona Bowie (Grand Rapids, Mich.: William B. Eerdmans Publishing Company, 1997), 24.

David Rensberger, "Thirsty for God," *Weavings* (July/August 2000): 20.

Michel Quoist, *Prayers*, trans. Agnes M. Forsyth and Anne Marie de Commaille (New York: Avon Books, 1975), 141.

Brother Lawrence, *The Practice of the Presence of God*, ed. Douglas V. Steere (Nashville, Tenn.: The Upper Room, 1950), 21.

Margaret Guenther, *The Practice of Prayer* (Cambridge, Mass.: Cowley Publications, 1998), 10.

Parker J. Palmer, *Let Your Life Speak: Listening for the Voice of Vocation* (San Francisco: Jossey-Bass, 2000), 4.

WEEK 2: CHANGING FROM THE INSIDE

Chittister, *Scarred by Struggle*, 51.

Robert C. Morris, "Enlightening Annoyances: Jesus' Teachings as a Spur to Spiritual Growth," *Weavings* (Sept/Oct 2001): 41.

Deborah Smith Douglas, "Border Crossings," *Weavings* (Nov/Dec 2002): 13.

Sue Monk Kidd, "The Secret of Winter Foliage," *Weavings* (Nov/Dec 2000): 15.

Downey, "Gift's Constant Coming," 29.

Henri J. M. Nouwen, *The Path of Peace* (New York: Crossroad Publishing Company, 1995), 23–24.

Underhill, *The Soul's Delight*, 14.

WEEK 3: LISTENING TO THE GROANS

Chittister, *Scarred by Struggle*, 16.

Ibid., 83.

Frederick Quinn, *To Heal the Earth: A Theology of Ecology* (Nashville, Tenn.: Upper Room Books, 1994), 61.

Quoist, *Prayers*, 29.

Joyce Rupp, *Your Sorrow Is My Sorrow: Hope and Strength in Time of Suffering* (New York: Crossroad Publishing Company, 1999), 97.

Nouwen, *The Path of Peace*, 14.

Ibid., 40.

WEEK 4: EXPERIENCING THE GOD WHO HEALS

John Claypool, *Mending the Heart* (Cambridge, Mass.: Cowley Publications, 1999), 43.

Ibid., 67.

Jean M. Blomquist, "The Close and Holy Darkness," *Weavings* (Jan/Feb 2002): 21.

Douglas, "Border Crossings," 15.

David Rensberger, "Suffering Together before God," *Weavings* (Sept/Oct 2002): 43.

Robert C. Morris, "Suffering and the Courage of God," *Weavings* (Sept/Oct 2002): 11.

Kidd, "Secret of Winter Foliage," 21.

Brother Lawrence, *Practice of the Presence of God*, 30.

WEEK 5: DISCOVERING COMMUNITY TOGETHER

Kristen Johnson Ingram, "Slowly Waking to Justice," *Weavings* (Nov/Dec 2002): 20.

Quoist, *Prayers*, 77.

Guenther, *The Practice of Prayer*, 192.

Elizabeth J. Canham, *A Table of Delight: Feasting with God in the Wilderness* (Nashville, Tenn.: Upper Room Books, 2005), 48.

Nouwen, *The Path of Peace*, 35.

About the Authors

Trevor Hudson is married to Debbie, and together they are the parents of Joni and Mark. He has been in the Methodist ministry in South Africa for over thirty years, spending most of this time in and around Johannesburg. Presently, he is part of the pastoral team at Northfield Methodist Church in Benoni, where he preaches and teaches on a weekly basis.

Trevor travels internationally and leads conferences, retreats, and workshops in diverse settings. He has written a number of books, including *A Mile in My Shoes: Cultivating Compassion,* published in 2005 by Upper Room Books.

Stephen D. Bryant is editor and publisher of Upper Room Ministries. His vision of small groups as important settings for spiritual formation and his experience in the contemplative life as well as in local churches provided the inspiration for the Companions in Christ series.

Before his election as editor and publisher, Stephen, an ordained minister and former pastor in The United Methodist Church, served as the Director of Spiritual Formation for The Upper Room and as the International Director of The Walk to Emmaus and Chrysalis movements.